iBRAND™

THE NEXT GENERATION

A guide to building the personal brand you desire to be:
A compilation of life lessons, stories and testimonials
honoring marketing & branding expert, the late Gary Sain
by

Pamela Sain & Olivia Sain

www.iBrandNextGen.com

THE NEXT GENERATION

ISBN: 978-1539122555

Credits

Editor	Kathleen Green, Positively Proofed, Plano, TX info@PositivelyProofed.com
Copy Editor	Caroline Bartholomew, 1caroline@comcast.net
Design, Art Direction, and Production	Melissa Cabana, Back Porch Creative, Frisco, TX info@BackPorchCreative.com

This book is dedicated in loving memory of
Gary Clinton Sain.

Beloved husband, loving father,
community leader, visionary, mentor
and friend to many.

Until we meet again!

We would like to thank
the industry leaders and friends
who contributed to this project.
Your stories will continue
to inspire future generations.

What People Are Saying...

"Gary Sain never let there be any doubt about what he stood for. The iBRAND should always come first in business and continue to be burnished. Gary lived and defined iBRAND based on honesty, authenticity and credibility. His iBRAND shines today – as bright as ever."

> – **Steve Moore**,
> President & CEO,
> Visit Phoenix

"Gary Sain made a huge impact on my family and me, and for that I will always be grateful. He was my boss, mentor and more importantly, my friend."

> – **Chuck Bowling**,
> President & COO,
> Mandalay Bay Resort & Casino

"My grandmother told me that small people talk about people, common people talk about things and smart people talk about ideas. Gary Sain was a very smart person. He was always thinking of great branding and how people could improve their brands. Most people in our business are still talking about people and we need to get back to talking about ideas."

> – **Brian D. Stevens**,
> CEO,
> Conference Direct

"Gary Sain is the genuine article. Gary's commitment to the hospitality and destination marketing industry is well documented and very much respected by his colleagues in the community. He has left a great legacy, but his presence will be missed for years."
　　　　– **John Graham**, CAE,
　　　　　President & CEO,
　　　　　American Society of Association Executives
　　　　　(ASAE)

"Gary Sain was the motivator, the believer, the disciple, the best leader for the organization and the best role model for public relations I have ever known."
　　　　– **Dr. Dan Holsenbeck**,
　　　　　Senior Vice President of University Relations,
　　　　　University of Central Florida

"Gary Sain was truly inspirational, engaging and extremely hospitable. These traits suited Gary perfectly as a Central Florida Tourism Marketing Ambassador."
　　　　– **Rich Maladecki**,
　　　　　President & CEO,
　　　　　Central Florida Hotel & Lodging Association
　　　　　(CFHLA)

"I can honestly say that I've witnessed some amazing orators in my time, but Gary Sain was one of the absolute best. He was a great leader, inspirational speaker and had a rare ability to convey memorable messages, good and bad, in a warm and passionate way."
　　　　– **Adrian Jones**,
　　　　　General Manager,
　　　　　LegoLand Florida Resort

Foreword

By Peter Greenberg, CBS News Travel Editor

We live in an often harsh and unforgiving, relentless world of branding, of product placement, of the worship of demographics all too often taking precedence over common sense. But most people tend to forget about how truly successful brands – and in particular, strong, credible personal brands – are built, developed and maintained.

Gary Sain knew all about that, because to him, it wasn't about the traditional metrics of brand management. His outreach was old school, and in the world of building a personal brand, he proved that old school is the best school.

I learned from Gary about how to be proactive without selling anything. It was all about basic people-to-people communication and follow-through. Gary didn't just call you. He kept in touch. He didn't start a conversation with an agenda other than to establish common ground. That conversation could be about a story he saw in the newspaper that you might be interested in; or to comment on a piece you had just done on the network. Or just to talk about an issue he found fascinating, funny, pathetic or absurd – or all of the above.

He practiced a basic rule I now follow religiously: The best way to get something is NOT to ask for it. There was nothing one-dimensional about Gary. My mother once told me that it was more important to be *interested* than interesting. I didn't fully comprehend the importance of that when she told me, but she was right. Mothers, as I later discovered, are always right. And, constantly being interested certainly defined Gary.

And that's part of what made him so effective. How could you not take his phone call when you knew that he always had something interesting to say? And the dynamic of those calls with me – and I presume just about everyone else Gary came in contact with – was that by the end of the call you were asking Gary what you could do for him. This wasn't a quid pro quo conversation. You just wanted to offer. And in the end, it was truly a win-win situation – not a carefully orchestrated, contrived formula or pop psychology technique or tool. It was just another special conversation with Gary.

When Gary died, it hit a lot of us hard, because there was suddenly a large void in those ongoing conversations that defined his friendships, and his personal brand. And those were the conversations that often guided us in the right direction. I was not alone in coming to grips with the hard reality that someone really special had left us.

I've tried to learn from Gary's approach to people. For many years now, each night before I go to bed I make a list of everyone I want to talk to the next day. There are usually about 60 people on that list. Of that number, only about 10 ever relate directly to ongoing projects or people I have to call. It's the other 50 on that call list that directly relate to how Gary lived his life. The majority of those folks on that list are there simply because I wanted to call them and say hello and keep in touch. No hidden agendas. I thank Gary for that. His efforts to constantly reach out, to talk to people, to *listen* are what so wonderfully defined him and became part of his personal brand.

A few years ago, I got a phone call saying I was selected to be inducted into the U.S. Travel Association's Hall of Leaders. It came as a total surprise. And then I learned I would be joined in the induction – posthumously – by Gary. My initial reaction – and it remains my reaction today – was that I wasn't going to be joined by Gary. Just the opposite. I was honored to be joining *him*.

Table of Contents

The Man Behind iBRAND

By Pamela Sain

On May 4, 2012, what seemed to be a normal day for Gary and me turned out to be a life-altering one.

Gary was the President & CEO of Visit Orlando and that position required extensive traveling, networking, public speaking and philanthropic contributions. So it was a typical Friday night for us. Gary was the chairman of the Celebrate the Children Gala for the Boys & Girls Clubs of Central Florida and was going to deliver the opening speech. I remember so vividly the smiles on the children's faces as he shook their hands and greeted them individually before his speech. He was in his element that night – full of energy, chatting easily and connecting with people in the room. Gary had an infectious smile that drew people in and disarmed them. As he approached the podium to give his welcome speech, I suddenly felt compelled to reach for my phone and record the address from beginning to end. The funny thing is, I usually never thought to do that because he gives so many.

Once again, Gary nailed it. He was authentic, gracious, humble, articulate, and he got to the point quickly and artfully. He walked off stage, came back to our table, ate his dinner and then leaned over to me and said, "Now I'm going to get my glass of red wine." He went for that glass but he never came back. I sat at that table for a long time thinking he was networking the room. It was quite normal for me to go to an event and not see him for a while because that was his opportunity to meet people and connect with them. As more time passed, I started to feel uneasy.

My phone rang; it was Gary. I picked it up but only heard background noise. I figured he had called me by accident – that was another thing he would often do. I tried calling him back but got no answer. I texted… still no answer. At that point, I contemplated getting up to go look for him, but the program was beginning to start and I thought he'd be right back.

A while passed and a woman approached our table and asked me if I was Mrs. Sain. I said I was. "You need to come with me right away," she said. I knew something wasn't right. As we walked out of the ballroom, I kept asking her questions. She remained silent. I was practically running down the hall when I heard a lot of noise and commotion ahead. As I turned a corner, I came upon a sight that nothing could have prepared me for. Gary was lying on the floor lifeless, surrounded by first responders in full-blown CPR mode, waiting for paramedics to arrive. I knelt next to him and felt for a pulse but there was none. The paramedics arrived and I was pulled away as they yelled, "Clear!" They shocked him with the AED, but there was no response. They continued to work furiously on Gary, but I knew in my heart of hearts he was gone.

At the hospital, our two daughters, friends and I were escorted to a consultation room – never a good sign. The room was eerily cold and quiet with no windows. Finally a doctor came in, and judging by the look on his face, the news wasn't going to be good. It was final. Gary was gone.

He died from myocardial infarction, which is a 70 percent to 80 percent blockage of the arteries. A piece of plaque had broken off causing a blood clot, resulting in sudden death. I was in complete shock and paralyzed with disbelief. It was as if he had been struck by a bus. No warning. No preparation. No chance to survive. I started to think about the things we had said and those we hadn't. There had been no goodbye.

I remember the night before Gary died. He and I were talking about the Rosen College of Hospitality Management and how important it was for him to continue donating his time to the school and the scholarship he established for his father, Frank. Gary and his father were the only father and son to have led the top three destinations in the country (Chicago, Las Vegas and Orlando.) As Gary thought about his father's career, he said to me that night, "I don't think people get what I do." I replied, "Unfortunately, people don't get what we do until we are gone and it's too late!"

We talked more about his father and mine, both of whom were cancer patients and lost their battles with the disease. Gary said, "I hope the day I go, it's so quick I won't know what hit me."

Two weeks prior to this conversation I had a nightmare that woke me from a deep sleep. It seemed so real I had a hard time at first distinguishing if it was, in fact, just a dream. I awoke sobbing and could feel my heart beating out of my chest. I could hear the television outside on the patio. I leapt out of bed and ran through the house to find Gary on the patio in his chair with his eyes closed and his chin resting on his hand with the TV blaring. He was so still. I threw the door open and called his name in a panicked voice. He woke up startled, wanting to know what was the matter and why I was crying. I told him I had dreamed he died of a heart attack, and in true Gary form, he replied, "What in the world did you dream that for?" He came inside to the kitchen and I explained the dream. He assured me he was fine and we talked and came to the conclusion that I had dreamed about his death because we had been talking about losing our fathers that night, too. Now I think it was a horrible premonition.

The day after Gary died, our daughters, Vanessa and Olivia, and I were still digesting what had happened. As if in a fog, we started making calls to immediate family members and set up an appointment with a funeral home. Then the press began calling. It turns out Gary was all over the television. We were later told that there had been a moment of silence in his honor at the Amway Center in Orlando, which was hosting the NBA finals. The news of Gary's death was even on the ticker tape of the national news. People from all over the country started calling to express their sadness. I began to rethink every conversation Gary and I had had that week and all I could hear over and over in my head was what he had said to me the night before he died, "I don't think people get what I do." I realized that in planning his wake and funeral, it would be important to select speakers who could articulate what my husband had built, how he had made a difference in the community and what his accomplishments were and meant. I wanted to make him proud.

Our house became a central planning station. We pored over transportation schedules, seating charts for dignitaries and VIPs and catering options. People helping with the planning and offering condolences came and went at such a pace that I had to hide in my closet at one point just to get five minutes of peace. There were so many details to attend to that we didn't even have time to grieve.

The girls and I met with our pastor, Joel Hunter, to discuss what kind of funeral service we wanted for Gary. It was important to us, we said, to keep his energetic and indomitable spirit alive and present. We wanted it to be a celebration of his life, which was truly a wonderful one. He traveled extensively, was a visionary, had real passion for what he did and never was too busy to be a true friend. He loved his two daughters. They were the reason he worked so hard. He loved rock 'n' roll, as well as a good Frank Sinatra song, and Lynyrd Skynyrd's "Free Bird" was a favorite. We gathered photos of Gary's life – personal shots of him with family members and professionals. We laughed about how he used to dress up in an orange Santa suit (ever true to promoting Orange County) with his assistant, Marie, as his chief elf. He and I used to say that while I was Gary's home wife, Marie was his work wife. It took both of us to keep him together. He was always on the go.

Truly, I don't know how he did as much as he did in a day or got from one place to another. He felt the need to be everywhere. He didn't want to disappoint anyone by not showing up. I used to joke with him, "You don't have to go to the opening of a letter!" Gary would laugh and sigh and fire back, "Pam, you would never make it in my job."

The wake began Friday, May 11 at 3 p.m., but people started arriving at 2. They were lined up out the door. Later someone told me the line snaked all the way to the street. The exit ramp, too, was completely backed up. I didn't know it then, but a lot of people couldn't find a place to park or weren't able to get inside.

As I stood there, it hit me that each of these many, many people came because they knew Gary and because he had really touched their lives. They wanted to tell their stories. They wanted to thank me and my daughters for sharing him with the hospitality industry and the community. I remember some of them cried and said they didn't know how they'd go on without Gary. Trust me, I understood! Still, it was so very surreal for me to see so many people truly grieving over Gary's death. This was definitely the moment that Vanessa and Olivia realized what a far-reaching impact their father had.

The funeral the following day was also a sea of faces. I was, again, humbled by the number of people who came from far and wide, from Gary's recent past and from having known him long ago, to pay their respects. Gary would have been astonished. A couple of times I would look over at the casket and think that at any moment he would sit up and say, "Oh, my God! I don't believe this!"

Gary was, above all, a humble man. And I knew that was exactly why so many people loved him. I remember talking to him a long time ago as we were walking to the Orlando Convention Center to attend the International Plastics Showcase and asking if he thought his name would be on a plaque here for having served as the President & CEO of the city's Convention and Visitors Bureau. He had laughed and replied, "Are you kidding?" He wasn't being sarcastic. As successful as Gary was, I don't think he ever stopped to give himself credit.

That's who he was. He worked hard because he loved it, not to promote himself. He thought of himself as a coach for his team and that's how he worked. If you were on his team, he wanted you to succeed in business and in life. If that meant losing you to another position or organization, he was the first person to offer encouragement. I don't know many people with that kind of unselfish confidence.

Gary also lived one day at a time. He never rested on what he had accomplished but strove to be better every day. "Don't ride on yesterday's accolades. You're only as good as today's work," he'd say.

As the days passed after the funeral, the girls and I continued to receive letters, cards and phone calls about how Gary had made a difference in these people's lives. There were more heartfelt stories. We could hardly go anywhere without someone stopping us to say they were happy they had known him and had loved or respected him. I had friends who had seen him the week before his death at World Travel Week who talked about how they now regretted having not stopped by his booth to say hello.

A week or so after the funeral, I received a call from a member of the U.S. Travel Association; they were planning a fundraising event in Gary's honor. I had already established the Gary C. Sain Endowment at the Rosen College of Hospitality Management, and the travel industry leaders wanted to form a steering committee for an event in Washington, D.C., to celebrate Gary's contributions and raise money for the endowment.

Roger Dow, President & CEO of U.S. Travel Association, shares that "even in his passing, his tribute raised money, and in true Gary fashion, brought people together and rallied to raise over $200,000 for the Gary C. Sain Memorial Endowed Scholarship for the University of Central Florida's Rosen College of Hospitality Management. That went to educate future industry leaders and carry on Gary's legacy and love for the travel industry."

Friends and colleagues of more than 40 years gathered that night and the tributes kept coming. I remember that at one point in the program a picture came up on the screen of our nation's Capitol flying the American flag at half-mast. **U.S. Sen. Marco Rubio** (R-Fla.) had ordered the flag to fly in Gary's honor that day. I have that flag still. Sen. Rubio conveys his thoughts:

66 Gary was more than just the President of Visit Orlando, he was a friend. Gary's work in Central Florida allowed him to touch countless lives during his time with us. He was a

devoted leader, mentor and visionary. Gary was passionate about the future of our children and their education. This was evident in the years he devoted teaching and advising others at the University of Central Florida's Rosen College of Hospitality and volunteering in Central Florida. Having the opportunity to work with Gary is one that I will never forget. His thirst for life and compassion for others was truly inspirational to witness. Gary's legacy will live on through his family and the lives he touched. "

I don't have the appropriate words to describe how I felt that evening. I was simply overcome. No one in Gary's family had ever received such an honor. I wished he could have seen the outpouring of appreciation.

As time went on, I tried to shake myself out of the fog I was in. For the 32 years we were married, Gary and I had experienced an exciting, nonstop schedule. Now there was silence. I knew I had to stay busy and be an example for the girls – to show them that Mom would be okay and that they had the rest of their lives to live. I needed a good reason to get out of bed in the morning, shower, put my clothes on and get out of the house. I was glad we had been active in many charitable organizations in the community and that I could continue to be involved that way. But I wasn't sure that was going to be enough.

Olivia and I found ourselves reaching for Gary, trying to find him in what he had written and said and what others had written about him. We spent hours rereading the condolence cards, looking up articles he had authored and watching YouTube videos of him speaking. We sorted through boxes we had packed with items from his office. We were particularly drawn to the articles he had written about iBRAND and delivering "WOW," as he dubbed it. He was all about standing out from the crowd and making a difference. Olivia began printing all of Gary's articles and filing them. One day, she came to me and said, "Mom, I hate to see all of dad's hard work sitting on a shelf, collecting dust."

Gary and I had talked at length about how, when he retired, he would speak, consult and write a book on **iBRAND**. I remember encouraging him to start that book in the months before he died. Of course, he responded by chuckling and saying, "Who is going to read that?"

That's when we started thinking, "What if we could continue telling Gary's story? What if we could keep him alive through his message, his words of wisdom and his positive spirit?" We certainly didn't have Gary's credentials, nor were we him, but we were the ones who had truly known him. And what better therapy for us than to pursue a new purpose for our lives inspired by Gary, a new project that brought us closer to him every day.

As Olivia and I got serious about spreading the word about Gary's **iBRAND** message, I realized the first thing we needed to do was secure the trademark he had on **iBRAND**. I had already started the Gary C. Sain Movement to Inspire, which raised money for the Boys & Girls Clubs and was built on Gary's **iBRAND** principles. That was the first step.

Next, we developed a website. Then we started using social media – Facebook, Twitter, Instagram and Pinterest – to test the waters and see if we would have an audience. We would post quotes from Gary's articles and elaborate on the messages. We began writing a blog with short articles explaining his theories and asking pointed, thought-provoking questions at the end. Now we were out of the gate and truly committed!

We had no idea how to gauge how many people we were reaching, but as we began receiving positive comments – from parents who shared our blog with their children, from managers who wanted their team members to read what we were saying and even some from people in foreign countries – we realized we were onto something big. We began having the articles translated into Spanish and Portuguese, and that's when the comments and visits went through the roof!

Managing the blog became a full-time job for Olivia and me. We learned how to track the number of visitors our blog attracted and saw that in one month alone we had 90,000 hits! We had no idea how this was happening and I really believe our inexperience helped us in this regard. We weren't trying to promote something or ourselves; we were passionate about our mission to get Gary's voice and ideas out there. That was all.

What is pretty amazing is that though we were neophytes in the social media world and in tackling this kind of project, what we were doing came so naturally to us. It was as if Gary was guiding us along. We would even dream about ideas, numbers, names that we could use in the blog. We were inspired and we were finding ourselves through the work. Olivia told me that by working on iBRAND, she had started to once again feel like the person she was before her father died. She missed him and she could hear his voice once again.

Olivia and I decided it was time to write the book that Gary didn't have time to do. iBRAND is a collection of Gary's published articles, notes, presentations and testimonials from friends and colleagues around the world. These chapters contain stories that are full of good life lessons that we believe are in danger of becoming obsolete. We hope Gary's legacy will inspire so many others to be the best they can be and enjoy work and life to the fullest.

In researching and publishing this book, we have come full circle. We have taken on his mantle because we are proud to be extensions of Gary and his brand. We always will be. And no doubt we always were.

iBRAND is a collection of Gary's published articles, notes, presentations and testimonials from friends and colleagues around the world. These chapters contain stories that are full of good life lessons that we believe are in danger of becoming obsolete. We hope Gary's legacy will inspire so many others to be the best they can be and enjoy work and life to the fullest.

If you would like to make a contribution to one of our scholarship funds, please make checks payable to:

UCF Foundation, Inc.

On the memo line, indicate which scholarship:

The Gary C. Sain Memorial Endowed Scholarship or
The Frank C. Sain Memorial Endowed Scholarship

12424 Research Parkway, Suite 250
Orlando, FL 32826

My Father, My Mentor

By Olivia Sain

"Always remember my two words to live your life by:
CHOOSE WISELY. Choose wisely in what you do.
Choose wisely when it comes to peer pressure.
Choose wisely in whom you're with. Choose wisely
based on how you were raised, right from wrong and
what you stand for. Remember, your reputation and
your standards must never be compromised."

— GARY SAIN

Most people would say their mentor is a professor, guidance
counselor, rock star, athlete, or reality TV star. For me, it was my
father. He was the extraordinary example I lived by every day.
His influence taught me right from wrong, and he was the role
model who showed me what hard work could get you. He was
my whole world and best bud. We had a very close relationship.
You would have had to know him to understand the person he
was. Words don't do him justice. He was handsome, charismatic,
a jokester, fun, optimistic, full of life and had an energy that was

infectious. He had a smile no one could duplicate and a distinct laugh, which you could pick out in a room full of thousands. He had a way of drawing you in. Whether he was working on a project or trying to come up with an idea, his persuasive manner made everyone want to be a part of his plan. He was about making everything fun. He truly had a gift when he was around people. His presence always left others feeling inspired. Maya Angelou said it best: *I've learned that people will forget what you said, people will forget what you did, but people will never forget how you made them feel.*

Learning to live when someone so important to you is gone is a difficult process. The pain is excruciating, the journey is lonely, and a feeling of darkness is inevitable. They say grief comes in stages. If that were true, then a stage would only occur once. Instead, grief is like a storm that comes and goes. Some days are calm, like a day of gentle rain, and others are like a turbulent storm. After the storm, you wait for the sun to shine and the sky to clear. Before you know it, here come the clouds once again and you are right back to where you started. Grief is like a season of constantly changing weather.

I was 23 when I lost my father. I was studying for my bachelor's degree at the University of Central Florida and working part time. My parents, having been raised in the Midwest with strong work ethics, felt it was important to instill the same in me as well as an appreciation for the value of each dollar earned. Most of my family came from a military background and also served in politics. This was a reason the bar was set high in our household. My father always thought he didn't meet his own father's expectations until he became the President & CEO of Visit Orlando. This forced him to constantly improve on his weaknesses and to strive to be better than he was the day before. *To never ride on yesterday's accolades. You're only as good as today's work.* He did all of this in his pursuit to be the best. He had to instill his own discipline. He expected the same from me because he wanted me to have the same opportunities in my future. Education was of No. 1 importance to him. He taught me how **knowledge is powerful**, and no one can ever take away your education.

After losing my greatest mentor, I struggled and lost hope in myself and my future. It was as if I was left in the middle of a desert with no map to find my way back. My father had been my compass and I had lost my source of direction. I was on a road to nowhere. The hardest part was not having anyone to talk or relate to because most of my friends' fathers were alive. I became more isolated. Solitude became my only friend. I suffered from major depression, anxiety, hospitalized for panic attacks and was on the verge of developing a drinking problem. I was struggling to hold my head above water.

Continuing my education was a struggle. I was not your average student. As a child, I had medical and educational challenges. When you grow up with Tourette's Syndrome and epilepsy, school and social interactions are difficult. My dad was my biggest cheerleader and taught me to never give up and never allow someone to tell me that I can't achieve something.

Going into my senior year at Bishop Moore Catholic High School, my parents were called in by the principal and guidance counselor to inform them that they didn't think I would successfully finish my senior year and I needed to look for another option. In true dad form, he replied, "That is not an option. Make it work!" My dad believed failure was never an option. After all the tutoring over the years, I went on to successfully graduating high school, receiving my Associate of Arts degree at Valencia Community College and am currently finishing up my bachelor's degree at the University of Central Florida. I remember my father always saying,

"As long as you get a college degree, I know I did something right." I knew how important it was to him. However, the year he passed away, I was not mentally ready to return to the university. I did anyway, which resulted into me getting disqualified for poor grades. On top of everything else, that was the straw that broke the camel's back. I didn't know how I was going to come back from that. It was the final disappointment. I was no longer in a standstill. I was in a black hole.

I needed something to pull me out of my darkness. I needed a purpose. I needed something to live for. I needed my father's wisdom and guidance. Not surprisingly, that proved to be the answer. Over the years, we had numerous talks at the dinner table about how people could be their best selves if they could think of themselves as a brand, and how optimism is the key factor to making their personal brand a success.

iBRAND Defined

"**What is a brand?** A brand represents the sum of all experiences over time between an individual, a company, a product, or a service. A brand represents an expectation, a level of quality, and it's a measure of trust. It's more than a logo. Products occupy a space on a shelf; brands occupy a space in your mind. Most of us are acutely aware of the concept of branding. It surrounds and influences our decisions every day.

"iBRAND is an attitudinal mindset in how we position ourselves to various targeted audiences. I am a firm believer that individuals can be brands. Not in the traditional consumer sense like Proctor & Gamble, but in a deeper one-to-one relationship with those whom you serve. How each of us positions ourselves within our individual enterprises, as well as the business community as a whole, dictates our future success. The same branding principles used in companies every day can be tailored to individuals who want to stand out from the crowd. If great brands are about relationships, then individuals have the greatest opportunity to brand themselves.

"iBRAND is based on three important core pillars: credentials, standards and style. It's taking the time to evaluate your individual progress toward your overall goals and making the proper adjustments within these three core building blocks.

"How well you execute your personal brand based on these core pillars will determine how your targeted audience perceives you. Your targeted audiences are individuals you want to influence. These are your customers, your boss and your peers, maybe others. These three core pillars of iBRAND help reinforce your personal brand's distinction, esteem, relevance, and awareness to these targeted audiences."

— Gary Sain

iBRAND was created by the late Gary Sain more than 20 years ago. As a leading figure in the travel, tourism and hospitality industry, Gary was not only known as a marketing and branding expert, but an expert for personal branding. The key is to think of yourself as a brand. It's about positioning yourself to reach your goals, creating a personal distinction, and crafting a road map to get you where you want to go. Gary was extremely passionate about this topic because it helped him achieve his goals and become a respected leader in the industry.

As President & CEO, Gary re-branded the Orlando Orange County Convention & Visitors Bureau to Visit Orlando. Gary led the organization that markets and sells the Orlando area as the No. 1 family destination in the world, and one of the top meeting destinations in America. His professional efforts led to

Orlando being the first U.S. destination to reach 50 million visitors, and earned him recognition as one of the 25 most powerful people by MeetingNews Magazine 2007 and 2008, Orlando's Most Influential Tourism Executive by Orlando Business Journal in 2008, the 50 Most Powerful People in Orlando's Hall of Power 2012, U.S. Travel Hall of Leaders 2012, Central Florida Hotel and Lodging Association (CFHLA) Charles Andrews Memorial Hospitality Award for Leadership 2012, the Convention Industry Council (CIC) Hall of Leaders 2014, International Association of Exhibitions and Events (IAEE) Lifetime Achievement Award 2012, Destination Marketing Association International (DMAI) Hall of Fame Award 2016 and the Dick Pope Legacy Award 2016.

Gary's accomplishments went beyond his professional life. He gave generously of his time by fundraising and volunteering for nonprofits. His peers remember his commitment to so much and to so many.

""Gary had an elegant presence and aura about himself. He developed his persona to position himself as distinct, respected, and yet fully confident in himself and his achievements. His personal **iBRAND** allowed him to engage the exhibitions industry in a major fundraising effort that resulted in raising $1 million to positively support and enhance the advocacy efforts that are still led by the International Association of Exhibitions and Events (IAEE). He was personally responsible for raising those funds, which lasted four years, and we are once again raising funds, in Gary's name, to continue his legacy.""

— **David DuBois**, President & CEO,
International Association of Exhibitions
and Events (IAEE)

Gary contributed a large portion of his time and energy to civic and community affairs. He served on the advisory council of the Federal Reserve Bank, Brand USA Marketing, the University of Central Florida's Rosen College of Hospitality Management, Board of Directors for Florida Citrus Sports, the Salvation Army, the United Arts of Central Florida, the Boy Scouts of America's Central Florida Council, the U.S. Travel Association, Central Florida Hotel & Lodging Association (CFHLA), the International Association of Exhibits and Events (IAEE), and many more.

"Gary served as the first non-board member to serve as the chair of Boys & Girls Clubs of Central Florida's annual Celebrate the Children dinner and gala. Gary led the event to record results, and he took his commitment as the chair very seriously. He opened new doors of opportunity for the organization and laid the groundwork for this event to be one of Central Florida's largest and most successful charitable events."

— **Gary Cain**, President & CEO,
Boys & Girls Clubs

—————

"Gary had an idea that a partnership with Visit Orlando, Golden Corral and the Orlando Salvation Army would be a great relationship! So it began. Gary and Visit Orlando became a wonderful sponsor and partner to the Salvation Army and Helpings From the Heart. Soon I spoke to Gary about joining the advisory board of the Salvation Army. Gary agreed and through his generous spirit, his time and his talents, he made a remarkable contribution to our Salvation Army and to the local community that the Army serves. As a community leader, Gary was instrumental in helping the less fortunate."

— **Eric Holm**, President & CEO,
Metro Corral Partners

"Gary had genuine compassion for those who were struggling. He was curious about homelessness and poverty, not in a voyeuristic way but rather approached it with a mindset of problem solving. He always wanted to know more. I can't help but wonder in these days since his passing how he might have influenced our community in addressing homelessness from a systemic approach. That was Gary's way. It was his brand and what a brand it was."

> — **Brent Trotter**, President & CEO,
> Coalition for the Homeless of
> Central Florida, Inc.

Gary graduated from Davis & Elkins College in West Virginia in 1973, receiving a B.S. degree in Business Administration with a minor in Marketing. He had the pleasure of working for five different industry segments: hotels, cruises, marketing, advertising, and the meetings/trade-show industries. The experiences in each were remarkable and provided him with additional insight he might not have achieved if he had stayed in one particular discipline. The professional curiosity he had for other industry segments in travel motivated him to expand his comfort zone. The same can be said for various positions within an industry. Many of us have worked in different departments or different companies. The richness of your personal brand is the distinction you offer your targeted audience through personal insight.

The Commencement Speech

One of Gary's proudest career moments came on Aug. 4, 2007, when he delivered the commencement speech for the graduating class of the University of Central Florida College of Business and the University of Central Florida Rosen College of Hospitality Management. He had given countless presentations and speeches over the years, but never one as important as this. It felt good, he had told me, that his hard work meant something, that it validated him and proved him worthy of being chosen to impart knowledge and wisdom to this group of young men and women who were about to set sail and take on the world. He was also a bit daunted. He knew this speech had to be relevant, leave a lasting impression and touch souls. He knew he had to give the speech of his life.

I watched as Gary entered the auditorium dressed in cap and gown with the procession of graduates. These students had worked hard over the years, some their whole lives, to reach this day, and Gary intended to make it even more memorable for them.

"As President/CEO of the Orlando Orange County Convention & Visitors Bureau, I do what I love to do every day. I represent over 113,000 hotel rooms, eight of the world's greatest attractions, the second-largest convention center in the United States, 5,000-plus restaurants, 92 golf courses, 1,400 CVB members, and a staff of 175 outstanding professionals.

"The industry I represent attracts 50 million visitors a year, generating over $30 billion to the local Central Florida economy. I have been in the travel industry for over 30 years, working in the hotel, cruise, trade show, and advertising industries. Through my career, I have lived in Chicago, Las Vegas, Kansas City, Omaha, Washington, D.C., Atlanta, and of course, this great city. It's been a terrific journey for my family and me.

"**And it's not over.**

"I can just imagine the dreams and aspirations circling within each of you: the dream of doing what you love to do, whether it's making a significant contribution to society, inventing the next Google, or being your own boss in your own company. Yes, it's such an exhilarating time pondering those dreams! And a time also filled with anxiety about what the future may hold.

"This great institution has provided you an excellent educational foundation for the rest of your life. How you prepare when you walk out these doors in the pursuit of your dreams is paramount.

"How do you know the career (path) in life you have chosen is the right one? How will you measure success? How can you gain insight today that will help you make the right choices in life and fulfill your dreams? And are you willing to take risks needed to be the best you can be?

"There is no risk in doing nothing...**other than doing nothing.** Remember, dreams are only dreams unless you can **drive** them to action.

"I would like to offer you something today that has helped me live my dream. I call it **personal branding.** You all know the compelling stories of how Starbucks and Nike branded themselves. Well, this is about how you brand yourself as a person. It's about positioning yourself to reach your goals. It's about creating a personal distinction. It's about crafting a road map for yourself to get to where you want to go. It's about authenticity, values and standards. It's about how you stand out from the crowd and how you deliver on your personal brand promises. And, most importantly, it's about taking calculated risks in life.

"As Woody Allen once said, 'Eighty percent of success is just showing up.' **I believe showing up is 20 percent.** *How* **you do it is 80 percent of success.** This 80 percent is what I call 'personal branding.'

"Everyone is a brand. Sure, names like Donald Trump, Bill Gates, Oprah Winfrey, and David Beckham are certainly recognizable. If you are really iconic, your brand is one name: Shaq, Shakira, Sting, Jay-Z, and Madonna. However, you are just as important. **In fact, today you are in the most enviable position of being able to build the brand you desire to be.** Your contributions to business, family and society are largely in front of you.

The Key Is to Think of Yourself as a Brand

"I am extremely passionate about this topic because I know it works. It has helped me reach my goals. I would like to leave you with **three key building blocks**...

First, Develop a LifePlan

"Do you realize most of us spend more time planning a vacation than we do planning our lives? What do you want to achieve in life? How do you want your life to be replayed when you are 90? Do you have a written plan to get there? Do you hold yourself accountable?

"Your LifePlan can be just a couple of pages on the brand I call 'You.' It's a living document, which may change many times based on your life. **Yes, life comes at you fast!** Expect the unexpected! As a famous sports celebrity once said, 'If you don't know where you are going, you might end up somewhere else.'

"Your LifePlan should address a time frame…say 5 years. I know it's difficult to look into the future. However, each of you should fast forward your thinking to 2012. Where do you want to be? What do you want to be doing? What lifestyle do you want? Will you be living your dream or getting closer to it?

"Build your LifePlan on where you want to be…**not where you are today.** Envision what you want to become. **Plan it and execute it!**

"A quote from Steve Jobs after he was fired at the age of 30 from the company he founded, Apple:

> 'I am convinced that the only thing that kept me going was that I loved what I did. You've got to find what you love. Your work is going to fill a large part of your life. The only way to be truly satisfied is to do what you believe is great work. And the only way to do great work is to love what you do. If you haven't found it yet, keep looking. Don't settle. As with all matters of the heart, you'll know when you find it. And, like any great relationship, it just gets better and better as the years roll on. So keep looking until you find it. Don't settle.'
>
> – Steve Jobs

Secondly, Have a Mentor

"In my case, I had many. Mentors are individuals who have your best interest at heart. They want you to reach your goals and, in many ways, can help you get there. They can add insight and advice on your LifePlan. For many of you, your family members have been your mentors, as well as your professors and guidance counselors. That should never change. As you go through life, you will add more. The best mentors are those who believe in you and provide honest, constructive advice.

"By the way, I have a saying: 'Don't believe your own press.' You need people around you who keep you grounded and tell it like it is. As good as Tiger Woods is, he constantly improves on his weaknesses. It would be easy for him to coast on his success. Not Tiger. He strives every day to be better than he was the day before.

"I have worked for five hotel companies, a cruise line, a worldwide trade-show company, a branding and advertising firm, and now a destination marketing organization. I have worked in sales, marketing and management positions, starting as a sales trainee and now as a CEO of the world's greatest travel destination.

"I did all of this in pursuit of my goal of being the best I can be – taking risks to better myself – the best personal brand I could be. I could have easily stayed in my comfort zone in the hotel industry. However, I want to look back on my life at 90 and have no regrets about lost opportunities. I want to say I did it my way. Having strong mentors has helped me achieve my goals and reach my full potential.

"My wife and I have been married for 27 years and she is my biggest mentor and cheerleader. I will tell you one thing...you don't move your family 10 times around the country without your partner believing in you!

"Most of us prefer speaking to listening. And, we tend to have selective hearing. Mentoring is only effective when you truly listen to what is being said and understand its meaning. You may elect to not accept what you hear. However, **perception is reality**. Regardless of how you think you come across, it is how others perceive you that will dictate how they will interact with you and what kind of influence you'll be able to generate.

"Yes, it's about you because it's your life. But, you cannot do it alone. Your success in achieving your dream is based on achieving it through others. Mentoring can provide insights on how your personal brand is being perceived.

Thirdly, Attitude

"The biggest threat to your success in life, no matter what you do, is the attitude of indifference. It's very disheartening for me to witness so many people racing through life uninspired or bored with what they do. They have no fire within their bellies. They accept mediocrity and the status quo. They spend a disproportionate amount of time doing something they don't want to do. It shows in their attitude, their performance, and everyone sees it.

"I believe attitude drives actions, actions drive results, and results drive lifestyle…whatever lifestyle you choose.

"Being positive and passionate about what you do are the biggest factors of attitude. If you love what you do, you will be happy, fulfilled and energized. It will be illustrated in everything you do…with everyone you meet.

"Lance Armstrong would not have overcome cancer and the odds of winning seven Tours de France without a positive, winning attitude. Jennifer Hudson, an 'American Idol' finalist, didn't achieve her dream of winning 'American Idol.' However, her positive attitude and her passion gave her the perseverance to go on and win an Academy Award for 'Dreamgirls.'

"Enhancing your personal brand always has risk. To grow, you must reach out of your comfort zone and become uncomfortable. By doing so, you overcome your fears.

"I stuttered terribly when I was young. I was extremely uncomfortable speaking to anyone, let alone a group. Today, as I address this assembly, it is a very special day for me. I'm doing something I thought I could never do as a young adult.

"You have to believe in yourself and put yourself out there no matter how uncomfortable it may feel. It's the only way of growing your personal brand.

"Remember, in life, there are many people who will try and convince you that you can't do or achieve something. They are energy zappers! Always surround yourself with energy providers. If you hear something often enough, you will believe it… whether it's positive or negative.

Reputation Is Everything

"I don't believe you should ever compromise your standards. Your integrity, values and beliefs greatly enhance how you are perceived. Keep in mind, in life, perception is reality.

"You can achieve anything in life if you work hard. Follow your dreams. Put them into action with a LifePlan. Surround yourself with people who care about you. Attitude dictates altitude. You can fly as high and as far as your dreams will allow.

Dream Big But Act Humble

"Don't over-promise. Always embrace your personal and family history. Be true to who you are. Deliver on your word consistently for it is one of the most distinguishable characteristics of your brand.

"Life is a journey. Each day builds on the day before. Stay focused on what truly matters in life. Without dreams, there would be NO Disney, NO iPhone, NO President of the United States, NO YouTube, NO man on the moon, and NO Harry Potter.

"Or how about Richard Ellenburg, a Camelot Elementary science teacher with an affinity for the guitar, who is also a rare two-time winner of Orange County Teacher of the Year award…first in 1988 and again this last February. Earlier this month, he was named the 2008 Florida Dept. of Education/Macy's Teacher of the Year and the first Orange County teacher to win the statewide honor. Truly, Mr. Ellenburg is living his dream. He has elevated his personal brand by being the best he can be.

"And how about Nikki Blonsky? A year ago, at age 17, Nikki was scooping ice cream at Cold Stone and singing for tips. She always dreamed about being on stage as a singer. She is a full-figured young woman…not your typical 'Hollywood' stereotype. She entered a worldwide search for the lead role in a musical. She fought for the part for over a year. She never gave up. Her attitude gave her the perseverance and fortitude to compete. Many of you will see Nikki in one of the hottest movies this summer… alongside John Travolta, Queen Latifah, and Michelle Pfeiffer. The movie is 'Hairspray.' When you see Nikki's performance, you will know the **power of dreams**. Her passion truly resonates on the big screen.

"We all have dreams. Today one of my dreams came true. Dreams make life worth living. **Today** is the first day of the rest of your life and the start of a wonderful and exciting journey. Be the best you can be in whatever you choose. **But choose wisely.** You can achieve anything with great passion and focus. **However,** be properly prepared! This great institution has provided you a compelling foundation. Now it's up to you.

"Dream it, plan it, and as a well-known brand would say, 'JUST DO IT!'"

chapter 2

Your Personal Brand Is Always on Display!

The text in this chapter is taken completely from Gary's published articles, except for quotes from peers and their introductory paragraphs.

Your brand is a reflection of who you are, what you do and how you do it. A few well-known individuals have done an excellent job in branding themselves. In fact, they have done it so well their enterprise is an extension of their personal brand. Walt Disney, Donald Trump, Steve Wynn, Richard Branson and Bill Marriott come to mind. There are many more. However, you don't have to be a founder or a CEO to be an individual brand. All you need is the determination, commitment, the focus to be the best at what you do and the passion to persevere. By doing so, you distance yourself from your competitive set and establish a standard of excellence, which sets you apart. You become memorable. You become your own brand.

Dr. Abraham Pizam, Dean at the University of Central Florida's Rosen College of Hospitality Management, can attest to Gary's own style of branding. Even today, his way of relating to others sets the bar high and still brings back fond memories.

66Your personal brand is more than your name, job title or what's written on your resume. It's how people feel when they think of you and what they tell others about you. This principle applies to any product, service or cause and it's the driving force behind the most successful brands in the world. That's why Gary's perspective on personal branding continues to be as relevant as ever, even as communication continues to get faster, easier and more interactive.

"While technology makes it easier to build your personal brand, your day-to-day interactions with others is what truly defines your legacy. As time passes, memories of projects, meetings, networking events and the like will fade, but your peers will remember what you stood for, what you believed in and how you made them feel. That's what iBRAND is all about.99

I feel anyone in sales, marketing and customer service have the greatest opportunity to differentiate themselves through iBRANDing. Customers buy people first. They want to build a personal (one-to-one) relationship with an individual, not necessarily the company brand they represent. Granted, we all represent a company's brand, but genuine, long-lasting relationships are driven at the individual level. The reason for the customer to believe (or not to believe) is how well sales, marketing and customer service professionals position themselves in the eyes of their customers. Secondly, how well they deliver on their personal brand promise.

Most of us are acutely aware of the concept of branding. It surrounds and influences our decisions every day. If great brands are about relationships and emotional connections, then individuals have the greatest opportunity to brand themselves. I am a firm believer that individuals can be brands. How each of us positions ourselves within our individual enterprise, as well as the business community as a whole, dictates our future success.

It's about standing out from the crowd!

- **Being unique/differentiated** – Am I able to stand out from the crowd? Do I offer a discernible difference?

- **Being relevant** – Am I standing out in a way that is meaningful to my customers/peers/boss?

- **Being credible/believable** – Am I able to tell a story in a convincing manner and consistently deliver upon my brand promise?

- **Being well regarded** – Am I running my business life and personal life in a way that builds respect and trust?

- **Being knowledgeable** – Am I knowledgeable about my company, my customers, my competition and my industry? Do the customers I serve know what I do?

These are the fundamental pillars your personal brand must be built and managed around. Strong personal brands maintain a competitive differentiation. They offer a solid, trusted base from which to initiate and/or respond to change. Change is forever constant within our business and personal lives. The mark of great personal brands is how they deal with change. Charles Darwin said it best: *The most powerful natural species are those that adapt to environmental change without losing their fundamental identity, which gives them their competitive advantage.*

Strong personal brands always deal from a pillar of strength. Their deep beliefs and unwavering commitment to what they stand for never change. Their advantage is their commitment to consistent behavior, which brings value to their stakeholders. A strong personal brand also clarifies choice. It limits and screens out non-complimentary options and competitive threats. Standing out through a distinctive, discernible difference is critical for proper positioning. If you cannot see the distinct differences your personal brand can offer, look harder!

Vince LaRuffa, Vice President of Resort Sales & Marketing at Universal Orlando Resort, agrees that consistent methodology and a well-thought-out approach were trademarks of Gary's own personal brand, which underscored his integrity. He shares his thoughts:

> "The great philosopher Aristotle said, 'We are what we repeatedly do. Excellence is not an act, but a habit.' Gary knew the value of consistency in effort, of building the right habits, of doing the right things and doing them well. His success was not an accident. He planned it. He worked it. He had an indefatigable passion for life, for his work, his family and his friends. I was lucky to have known him and to learn from his example. This is his legacy."

How does one properly position oneself? It first starts with the right attitude. Attitude will determine altitude – how high you can soar. No personal brand can ever maximize its true potential without the right attitude. When it comes to fully understanding your personal brand position, check your ego at the door. You need to be clinically analytical and look at everything with an unbiased, open mind. Next is research. Not research you purchase. This is research you do yourself. First, you need to differentiate yourself in three market places: 1) within your company; 2) within your industry; and, 3) within your targeted audience(s). You do this by gaining insight into what the needs/desires of these respective audiences are and becoming exceptionally relevant to them. You learn what is critically important to them. Secondly, you create a personal brand position based on the strengths and weaknesses of all your stakeholders, competitors and company associates.

Positioning **iBRAND** is focusing on your skills. You cannot be everything to everyone. No individual can position himself/ herself as anything. I would suggest creating your own positioning statement by answering these questions:

1) Who are you?

2) What business are you in?

3) What people do you serve?

4) What are the special needs of the people you serve?

5) With whom are you competing?

6) What unique benefits does your customer or supervisor derive from your service?

In addition, consider asking others how you are honestly perceived. The most important [thing you can do] is know where you stand with your company brand in the minds of your targeted audience. It's extremely hard to be relevant or meaningful to your audience if you don't have this insight. Your personal brand is no different. You need to access how your audience perceives you. Perception is the key word. All of us think of ourselves differently than those around us. Ask your customers, family, friends, peers and industry associates to help you paint a picture of your personal brand. Only then, from insight, can you build on the building blocks to enhance your brand positioning and delivery.

As importantly, you build upon the quality traits of your personal brand, which you deem as distinctive. For example:

- Returning all phone calls within four hours;

- Answering all correspondence, including email within 24 hours;

- Sharpening your presentation skills in order to achieve more speaking opportunities;

- Mentoring junior staff members; and,

- Taking the initiative to develop one new idea per quarter.

The list is endless. The key is delivering your brand promise through distinctive activities/results that reinforce your individual brand position. This creates a discernible difference for your personal brand and allows you to rise to the very top of mind awareness within your targeted audience. The secret is identifying what your key discernible difference is that **cannot be easily duplicated!** Jerry Garcia said it best: *Don't be the best at what you do, be the only one at what you do.*

Knowledge can be one of the most distinctive discernible differences. Your insight into your company, your industry and your customers is a huge value proposition you can leverage. Anyone can identify problems. Personal brands that stand out are those that offer solutions. Having the skill set to effectively identify and develop solutions is based on insight and knowledge. A fundamental building block in leveraging your personal brand is to never stop learning – whether it's pursuing a master's degree, an accreditation, continuing education courses, industry networking events, trade and business publications, etc. Great personal brands never think they know it all. Their commitment to always being the best is what sets them apart.

Trust is a keyword often associated with branding. The ability for a customer to trust a brand because of past experiences/ associations and purchase again is the essence of great brands. Delivering on the brand promise every time is the reason to trust. Your personal brand is no different. Your word is your brand. Your behavior supports your word. Your positioning supports your behavior. Meeting and exceeding the expectations of your customers, your superiors and all other stakeholders is consistently delivering upon your brand promise. Only then is there a reason to believe.

Lastly, how do you know when your personal brand is in need of [re]vitalization? Here are some thoughts:

- Have you strayed away from your core beliefs?
- Do you have a well-established identity?
- Have you lost your edge?
- Has your performance slipped?
- Are you on top of your industry trends?
- Are you in touch with your customers and their wants and needs?
- Have you been outmaneuvered or become outdated by competitors or peers?
- Do you continue to differentiate yourself in a changing, competitive marketplace?
- Do you have the elasticity and strength to succeed in an ever-changing world?
- Are you consistent in your business relationships?

If anyone understood Gary, it was **Tim Hemphill**, Vice President of Sales & Marketing at the New Orleans Ernest N. Morial Convention Center. Their upbringings were strikingly parallel.

> "Gary and I had similar backgrounds in that our fathers both were in the industry and we grew up knowing nothing else. We both returned to our dads' respective roles in the industry, his at a convention and visitors bureau and mine in a convention center after each having had successful careers on related paths.
>
> "Gary was about 'the brand' and 'your brand' before it was mainstream. He understood and inspired others to recognize that you shouldn't feel awkward or selfish for wanting to develop your personal brand. It actually was a responsibility to be successful and to the success of your company. Unlike any other person I know, Gary could forge relationships and build relationship bridges faster and better than most, and I believe it is because of the unselfish attention he paid to his brand."

In today's competitive marketplace, branding is occupying a distinctive (favorable) space in the minds of your targeted audience. iBRANDing ensures you are occupying the right space for the most important brand: **YOURSELF!**

chapter 3

The Authentic You

pur·pose – *the reason for which something is done or created or for which something exists.*

For months after Gary's wake, many shared how he had touched their lives. And the stories kept coming. When we set out to write this book, we never would have imagined that even more wonderful stories would be shared with us at our request. Those stories are included in these pages. At times, the project seemed daunting. It was a constant reminder of what we had lost, but we wanted to keep Gary's work alive. That was our purpose. Stepping out of our comfort zone was hard, but in the process it made us stronger. We accomplished things we never imagined. To reach success, we had to define a vision, turn our ideas into action, raise the bar for ourselves and go for it.

We heard many stories of how meaningful Gary's friendship was to countless people. They felt as though he was their personal friend. How he impacted so many people would have astonished him. I truly believe it was because he was so passionate about what he did. His purpose was driven by being impactful, getting results and making a discernible difference. As the stories kept coming, we yearned to hear Gary's advice again, but this time it was through the voices of others. These individuals became the conduit to bring the messages back to us full circle.

Even after all the accomplishments and many accolades, there was still something missing in Gary's life. In the early years, our faith was important to share with our children. We always believed it's not about showing up on Sunday for church, but how you live your life seven days a week. Gary always taught the girls that if you talk the talk, you better walk the walk! In pursuing your purpose, you lead by example.

As we get older, we have more years behind us than ahead. You begin to question your faith and spirituality.

Two weeks before Gary's death, he had scheduled a lunch with our pastor, **Joel Hunter**. It was not unusual for them to meet from time to time, but this lunch was different. Dr. Hunter, Senior Pastor at Northland Church, remembers their conversation well:

> "Gary Sain was one of the most energetic, focused, and 'Let's get it done' people I've ever met. Orlando was fortunate (in my world, we call it 'blessed') because Gary literally brought a 'fortune' of visitors and spending to our region as the CEO of Visit Orlando. His marketing genius, his winning personality, contagious enthusiasm, and his team-building attitude brought hundreds of millions of people into our community. I knew him as a fellow community leader; Gary was interested in connecting with my network of religious leaders. He was also a friend who came with his wife, Pam, to the church

I serve as pastor. Gary always was interested in helping others toward their personal best. But in what proved to be the end of his life, he was interested in being helped toward his personal best – including his relationship with God.

"The Easter Sunday morning before he died, he came up to me in the midst of the crowd and said, 'Let's get together for lunch.' I'm sure he had said that a thousand times before to as many people; it wasn't the first time he said it to me. But there was something different in his voice that day – something that told me this would not be mainly about business or merely about networking.

"As we sat down at our table, Gary's demeanor was softer, more restrained than usual. He typically was full of energy, but today he was more reflective. I asked him how his life was going. We started with the usual business chatter, but even before we ordered our food, he told me his father had died and it was having a big impact on him. Pastors know when they have entered onto holy ground in a conversation. I simply said, 'Tell me about that.'

"He spoke in respectful, almost reverent tones about his father. There is a kind of love that straddles respect and warmth that humbles the one who loves. As he continued to talk on that day, he seemed to grow uncomfortable. It is normal that when someone we love dies, we are caught between gratitude for what was and regret for what could have been. Gary went deeper that day in our conversation, and I know he wouldn't mind me sharing with you the essence of what he said, because it was about a subject he dwelled on with everyone: being your best self.

"Gary was a family man, pure and simple. His eyes lit up when he talked about his wife, Pam. He knew he'd gotten the treasure of a lifetime with her. As Proverbs 31:10 reads, 'An excellent wife who can find? Her worth is far above jewels.' Gary was crazy about Pam. He was thankful not only for her love, but for her capable partnership and support. It is rare to find one overachiever married to another overachiever, but in Gary and Pam's case, that is exactly what happened. He talked about her every time we had an extended conversation. A lot of guys, when I ask, 'How's your family?' simply reply, 'Fine' or 'Good.' Gary usually went into some detail about Pam's strengths.

"But on this day, perhaps because he had just lost his own father, he dwelled on his daughters, Vanessa and Olivia. Again, his eyes lit up. It was easy to see his gratitude and love as he described each briefly and proudly. Yet, there was some regret, too. He was wondering if he had failed them as a religious influence. He said, 'You know, Vanessa used to have such a vibrant faith. She was involved at Northland, but it went deeper than that. It was central to her life for a while, and it's not anymore. I'm wondering if that's my fault.' He paused. He wasn't looking for reassurance or forgiveness; he was examining the place of faith in his own life. Our children tend to remind us what's really important in life. His father's death, his daughter's change, and perhaps the pace of his own life had him looking more deeply into what matters eternally.

"There is a deep place in our souls, sometimes skipped over for a time in the most zealous and active people, who can tend to substitute 'getting things done' or having 'over-the-top' moments with family and friends. Gary's love of his father, and his love of his family, had driven him to examine his spiritual condition at this time in his life. It is possible that in some deep reaches of his mind, he sensed what was coming, not just eventually but soon.

"He went defensive for just a moment. 'I'm not a church-every-Sunday kind of guy, but I live it, dammit!' I started laughing – not in derision, but because it was so…Gary. And then he smiled, and softened, and said quietly but plainly, 'I want a better relationship with God.' I said, 'Let me help with that, Gary; it's what I do.' He said, 'Thanks.' Then quickly offered the disclaimer, 'Now, I'm not going to be in church every week!' I started laughing again. It was just a start, but God already had him at 'Let's get together for lunch.'

"A short time later, he was gone from us to the God to whom he wanted to be closer.

"Gary was a great example of encouragement and accomplishment in this life. He may have been even a better example as he approached death. We all have only a certain number of days, and none of us knows when our time on earth will be finished. Gary had a remarkable impact on his family, and his city. Gary made the best of all possible turns toward the end, a turn toward the heavenly city. Hebrews 11:16: 'But as it is, they desire a better country, that is, a heavenly one. Therefore God is not ashamed to be called their God; for he has prepared a city for them.'"

Our sense of purpose is key to success. Purpose is a powerful word. For some it's a vital part of living, to feel that you bring something positive to the world in which we live. Sometimes our purpose can be driven by a family member who has left us in an untimely manner. This event redirects our lives to have a deeper meaning. We might feel as though their journey was not completed and there was still much to be accomplished.

Purpose gives us direction. It begins a path and journey we may not have ever imagined. We have all heard the saying, "When one door closes, another door opens." It's all about the first step you take into that new door. Don't walk blindly. Instead, open your eyes to the opportunities that surround you. It all goes back to how you observe whether the glass is half full or half empty.

▓ What do you want from your life?

▓ Why do you work?

▓ What drives you?

---

goal – *the object of a person's ambition or effort; an aim or desired result.*

One of the most important activities we take for granted or don't aggressively challenge ourselves with is personal goal setting. On a piece of paper, write down your goals for your life. Don't just include business goals; include community and family as well. They all interact. Life is not one-dimensional. I know this sounds somewhat philosophical. However, it's a good time to re-connect with yourself to reconfirm if you are still centered on the right things.

With hectic work and lifestyles, we sometimes forget why we are doing what we are doing. It is certainly for more than just paying the bills. You should always be questioning and reconfirming your goals.

▓ Where do you want to be in 5 years? In 10 years?

- What career path?

- What is the perfect job for you?

- If you didn't do what you currently do, what would you be doing?

- What do you want to do for your community, your church, etc.?

- What are your financial desires?

- Family aspirations?

- What do you want to be remembered for?

The questions are yours. The answers are priceless. This is a critical step within **iBRAND**.

Once you have this outline, write down your educational strengths and weaknesses. Do the same with your experiences and insights. What is missing to get you where you need to go? Where are the gaps? Highlight the additional education, experience and insight you need to help you achieve your goals. Then build a plan to fulfill your personal brand's extraordinary potential. Finally, it's all about relevance. Develop your plan to pursue your goals with your targeted audience in mind.

- What do you want to achieve?

- What do you want to create?

- What are your dreams?

val·ue – *a person's principles or standards of behavior; one's judgment of what is important in life.*

Our dinner table was always a place to teach our children in a non-intimidating setting. It helped form strong bonds and was always a place to meet their friends. You learn a lot about people when sharing a meal. Gary mentored many of our daughters' friends without knowing how important those messages would be later in life. The most frequently asked question was, "Did we bring value to the day?" Gary was all about having a Plan A and Plan B in case Plan A didn't work out. In some cases, you needed Plan B to support Plan A; granted, most adults don't have either. I think this message was engrained in our girls from the earliest age.

I think maintaining friendships was hard for our girls because most people did not meet their expectations. There was a strong example set in the family coming from a background of political leaders and military. The bar was set very high early on. I always expected our girls to try their hardest and do their best. Whereas Gary was always pushing it a bit further. If one daughter brought home an "A," he would ask, "Was there extra credit?" I know what you're thinking; 'This is one hard man to please!' But the message was that you can always do more. I believe that is what made Gary a success. He knew there was always room for improvement. He never expected a perfect review without new goals in place to exceed the last. Now, for some people this might be exhausting, but we never looked at it that way. I can assure you; this is what helped us write this book.

'Behind Every Successful Man Is a Woman'

Steve Feder, CEO of LIONFLEET, LLC, met Gary through a mutual acquaintance in 1983. Not only did Gary quickly win Steve's professional admiration but garnered a solid friendship, which grew to encompass Gary's family, as well. He recalls those first days and the ensuing years.

"Actually, I was in the midst of developing a young leadership group in Chicago, called Chicago's Fifth Star, comprised of young, rising business leaders, and one of the women on our fledging committee recommended I meet Gary Sain. She said we had a lot in common. Indeed we did. In fact, Gary, Pam and their children remained dear friends of ours from then on. I still count Pam and her children as some of my dearest friends.

"It was not surprising to me that Gary's career carried him to the pinnacle of his industry. He was one of the most ambitious, energetic and hard-working guys I knew. But Gary had another important quality that, I believe, contributed to his success. He was nice. He was one of the most considerate people I ever met. He never had a harsh word for anyone. He was supportive of the efforts of others and generous with his compliments.

"Pam was truly the great woman behind the great man. I remember first meeting Pam at the Tremont Hotel. Gary was the Vice President of sales and marketing for the property and invited me for lunch. Pam was shopping downtown and stopped by our table to say hello. I felt like I had known her all my life. She was warm, friendly, engaging and had the greatest sense of humor. It was clear that Gary and Pam were a matched set. It was obvious that they adored each other. There was almost a George Burns and Gracie Allen vibe to their banter. They had fun together, and all of their friends and family had fun just being in their presence.

"Pam and Gary worked as a team. They supported each other 100 percent of the time. The Sains must have moved 15 times in support of Gary's career, and Pam worked tirelessly in preparing the family for each move. Gary was an exceptional husband and father. He was a very involved father to Olivia and Vanessa. When we would meet, the first half of our get-together would be consumed with our discussion of the kids. He would tell me how they were doing in school and took great pride describing all of their extracurricular activities.

"Gary was a solid family man. I believe that he was respected by his business colleagues for many reasons (i.e., hard work, attention to detail, creativity, etc.). However, above all, I believe his colleagues respected him because he always found the time to be an active and involved husband and father. His presence was felt in the home, and Pam and the girls enjoyed a rich and rewarding home life because of Gary's very active participation.

"When I think about my dear friend Gary Sain, I had the great honor to watch him grow and succeed in his chosen profession. But what really stands out in my mind, and I continue to carry with me, was his generous spirit, kindness and his great devotion to his family and friends. I miss him and think of him often. He will always be an inspiration to me."

I believe the best present you can give someone is your presence. Time invested in friendship is priceless. People come into our lives and sometimes we don't see the value at the time, but the spirit of that love and respect lives on forever.

'The Winning Formula'

Maurice Arbelaez, Corporate Director of Sales & Marketing at Millenium Management Corporation, discusses the man behind the brand. While working closely with Gary on the board at Skal International's Orlando chapter, Maurice got a glance into the genius that was Gary Sain.

"A myriad of mixed feelings come to mind while sitting down to attempt to put into words and in few lines sharing my personal experiences from a brilliant marketer but especially a great friend, father and husband.

"Although I had the opportunity to travel with Gary on several occasions, I never really had the chance to get to know him more like a friend than a colleague. It was not until he became more involved with the Skal International Orlando chapter, working closely with him on the board, that I had the opportunity to know what Gary Sain really was all about.

"In my role of Vice President on the board, I learned many great things about Gary. His creative mind and knowledge of branding really opened a new dimension not only for me personally but to all of us on the board, highlighting that branding is directly linked to success.

"But in reality, all his attributes came as one whole package that combined many key factors that made up the needed ingredients to create 'True Branding': Vision, Creativity, Values, Trust, Purpose, Passion, Integrity, Ethics, Reputation and Attitude, among others. These could not have been possible without the support of a special family that was the backbone of his great qualities.

"Gary had a special passion for his beloved wife, Pam, but I could see in his eyes a spark when he spoke about his daughters, Vanessa and Olivia. These special individuals were the fuel for his drive and gave him the purpose and courage to seek excellence in whatever he set his mind to do.

"I remembered one day after a board meeting sitting with Gary to discuss my upcoming President position with Skal International Orlando as Gary generously indicated his commitment to support me as my Vice President. At that point, due to commitment and involvement in the business development with my company and ownership, I recognized that I was not going to be able to give my 100 percent of commitment to the board as its President, so I indicated to Gary that I thought the board and our chapter would benefit more from his direction.

"Although I decided to give up my presidency so Gary could become our next President, I never regretted my decision, because in reality I gained a very valuable experience by learning what I know today, not only about Branding, but what it really takes to put together all of these great qualities that Gary had and use them as a winning formula.

"I am very proud to say that I managed to get to know a great human being who despite his work being very important for him, he was always quick to say that his success was a result of his own important support system in life: an awesome family!

"I am also proud to say that Gary was my friend and colleague and that he truly represented what we in the hospitality world always strive for. He left us all too early, but his legacy will always live in our hearts and our industry."

Values play a pivotal role in your success at home and work. If you have a supportive partner and a happy, stable environment, you are able to carry those values out into the community. This allows you to be the best you can be in your career. This is vital to the value of your personal brand.

- What do you hold to be true?
- What's important to you?
- What are you willing to do and not do?

chapter 4

Credentials
(Why You Are Believable)

In the fall of 2006, Gary was working for a large advertising and public relations firm. The girls were in their late teens attending high school and college and I was a stay-at-home mom after retiring from having my own business doing calligraphy and special events for more than 20 years. Though Gary traveled a lot for work, we got to spend a good amount of time together.

Gary came home one night and told me he was interested in the CEO position that had just opened up at the Orlando/Orange County Convention & Visitors Bureau. This was a job like no other. If he got it, he would be responsible for everything that had to do with the No. 1 family tourist destination in the world! I knew we had a lot of talking to do. Gary's father, Frank, had headed the Chicago and Las Vegas convention bureaus for a little over 20 years, so Gary and I knew all too well what kind of pressures and time commitments would come with the job.

Already having planned a Thanksgiving family vacation to Charleston, S.C., the four of us used the six-hour car ride to go over the pros and cons of Gary taking this job. We knew it would affect all of us and we wanted to understand what we would all be getting into.

The negatives were first and they were many: Gary would be in the spotlight all the time; his every move would be scrutinized (although the CVB is a private company, the CEO is responsible for tourist development tax dollars); there would be a huge number of people to please – the mayor of Orange County, the mayor of Orlando, board of directors, over 1,400 CVB members and top-tier executives for theme parks and major attractions, not to mention a very large CVB staff itself; the press would always be watching, waiting to pounce if he took a wrong step; his family members, mainly Vanessa, Olivia and me, and even our family values would also be exposed to criticism and public attention; and he would definitely have less time to spend with us – there would always be an event to attend, a speech to make, a group to greet, a reason to go.

Next up, the pros. Gary would be the brand ambassador of the Orlando destination! The thought hadn't been on his radar at all. Up until now, that is. It would be the challenge of his life, but having worked in five industries (hotel, cruise, marketing, advertising, and meetings/trade shows) that could enrich a leadership role at Orlando's Convention and Visitors Bureau, he was eager and more than willing to go for it. We told him he could count on us, too.

So, now the preparation and hard work for Gary to land the job began. All that Thanksgiving weekend, we compiled lists of who's who in the industry and of colleagues and associates in the travel and hospitality businesses. Gary gathered statistics from all over the world that tracked visitation numbers, marketing campaigns and travel trends. He made hundreds of phone calls to understand all the challenges he could face if he became the CEO. The more he researched, the more he realized what taking the job would mean and that, yes, he was not only prepared to take the reins, but thoroughly excited about how he could take things to the next level.

There were countless rounds of interviews, and after each one, Gary did even more research. As he cleared each hurdle and moved up in the process, he told us that he wanted the position badly and was already working on his vision for Orlando's tourist industry and how he would implement it in case he was chosen.

Needless to say, Gary was offered the CEO position, and he went on to prove that he was not only a good choice but an ideal one.

Gary had many gifts, which **Mike Gamble**, President & CEO of SearchWide, was privy to when Gary was recruited for the President/CEO job with the Orlando Convention and Visitors Bureau. To this day, Mike is in awe of Gary's 2006 interview, which showcased meticulous preparation and a knack to put everyone in the room at ease.

Here is how it went, in the words of Mike Gamble:

'The Only One in the Room'

"The executive search business provides countless opportunities to meet simply amazing people and develop lasting relationships. When you couple that with a primary practice area in the travel/tourism/hospitality and events industry, the inspiring connections are magnified tenfold.

"I really got to know Gary in 2006, when I was trying to recruit him for the President/CEO position with the Orlando Convention and Visitors Bureau. We knew each other prior to that but did not have a business or personal relationship. In the search business, we depend on referrals from other trusted executives. Doug Price, who was working for Destination Marketing Association International (DMAI) as Executive Vice President at the time, highly recommended that I call Gary about the Orlando job. Thank you, Doug!!

"Gary's background was unique and nontraditional, yet perfect to run one of the largest Destination Marketing Organizations in the world. The first 30 years of his career consisted of sales and marketing leadership positions in various industry segments, including hotels, cruise, exhibition/events and a marketing/advertising agency. Gary, however, was not an easy recruit and he definitely played hard to get.

"The first call to Gary was in October of 2006 and he was slightly interested at best. His exact words were, 'I am just not sure that I want to be the CEO of a CVB.' For those who are not aware, Gary's father was the CEO of the Chicago and Las Vegas CVBs, so he knew better than anyone what the job entailed. He left the door open for more dialogue, but I knew that he was by no means 'all in,' so a face-to-face was a must.

"There were many unsuccessful tries to calibrate our schedules, so I asked him for his travel schedule and saw Los Angeles, mid-November. I told him that I would also be in LA at the same time. Years later, Gary and I laughed about the fact that he knew all along I had no intention of being in LA that week. He was right. It was a special trip to spend a couple of hours with him.

"Gary was still non-committal, even after our face-to-face, but he gave me the okay to 'float his name.' It was a very smart way to approach a high-profile position such as this, in order to maintain confidentiality, and to get a sense if the hiring party had any interest at all. The interest was there and Gary then asked if he could meet informally with a couple of the key search committee members, including the chair and chair-elect. Another great strategy to get some initial questions answered and continue to gauge the mutual interest before committing.

"On Dec. 1, 2006, Gary called me to say that he was 'all in' and that is when his focus and pursuit started. Those who knew Gary knew that when he put his mind to something, he went after it with everything that he had. By the time the formal interview came around, in late December, he was more prepared than anyone I have ever seen. I was actually worried that he was too prepared and encouraged him to carefully sprinkle his research and knowledge on the committee.

"Gary's interview with the committee was inspiring and, to this day, it is still one of the most memorable interviews that I have ever been a part of. He was, of course, impeccably dressed and he was immediately comfortable with the interview committee.

"Gary had a way of getting his message across in a concise, thoughtful and humble manner. His interpersonal skills were exceptional, in a boardroom or a crowded ballroom, and he made you feel like you were the 'only person in the room.' It was immediately clear that not only did he have the ability to run the organization but that his human skills would work exceptionally well with the multiple stakeholder groups and the elected officials.

"It was clear when he left the room that he had hit a homerun. Gary was his biggest critic, so when I walked out with him, he immediately said, 'How did I do?' I just smiled and said, 'Pretty sure you nailed that, Gary.' John Marks, retired CEO of the San Francisco CVB, was working with me on this search and said in the hall, 'That was one of the best interviews I have ever experienced.' I felt the same, and the search committee did as well.

"Gary immediately proceeded to the final stage in the interview process, which included one more interview with the committee and a few face-to-face meetings with elected officials and important stakeholders. As expected, he continued to do well and exceed expectations, and an offer was extended.

"We all expected Gary to do well as the CEO of the organization. What we did not expect was how quickly he would become an industry leader nationwide. The travel/tourism and Destination Marketing industry quickly began to recognize Gary as a humble and charismatic thought leader."

In Gary's Words:

Credentials make you believable. Credentials consist of education, experience and insight. It is the main reason why you were hired for your current position. At one time, you demonstrated to the appropriate individual(s) you have the skill set to perform your current job responsibilities better than anyone else. Your ability to continue to perform at a high standard determines if you can manage additional responsibilities in the future. Constantly updating your credentials can enhance your position in the minds of your customers, supervisors and peers. It promotes believability and credibility. It demonstrates you are committed to self-improvement. More importantly, it reinforces your desire to be the best at what you do and what you can do.

chapter 5

Lessons From a Mentor

The text in this chapter is taken completely from Gary's published articles, except for quotes from his business colleagues and two lead-in paragraphs.

Do you have a mentor? Oddly, most of us don't. Or, we may have had one at one time. If you are committed to improving your personal brand performance, you need a mentor. There is no age limit to having one. Everyone can use a mentor. A mentor can help you see your future path more clearly. He or she can provide valuable insight about you. A mentor can, if you are willing to listen, tell you what you may not want to hear regarding your personal brand positioning. To me, that's the most important insight a mentor can offer. Receiving constructive input is critical. Mentors, like coaches, can help you be the best you can be.

Gary was all about helping others. **Don Welsh**, President & CEO of Destination Marketing Association International (DMAI), saw the direct impact Gary had within their industry:

> "A true ambassador and mentor to so many in our industry. Gary Sain has left an indelible mark on the U.S.

visitor industry. His diverse background, zest for life and kindhearted disposition contributed to his uncanny ability to mentor, inspire and persevere. Our industry is stronger today because of him. 99

Who can be a mentor? Maybe it's your spouse, good friend, colleague, former boss, parent, etc. This list is endless. The key is to pick someone whose opinion you completely trust; someone who is committed to your overall success and happiness; someone who sees your personal brand as something special and is willing to help you unlock its full potential. Lastly, someone who is not afraid to tell you what you might not want to hear in order to be better tomorrow than you are today. If you don't have a mentor, I recommend finding one. Mentors can provide you unbiased coaching, which is critical for personal branding. In fact, your mentor is really your personal brand manager. Every brand has one. Why shouldn't the most important brand in the world – you – also have one?

Here is an example of how Gary's mentoring influenced others. **Jake Palm**, Assistant Night Manager at JW Marriott Marquis Hotel Dubai, shares his story:

"When asked if I would be willing to write about Gary's mentorship and about what he taught me, I had so many different thoughts and emotions. How would I be able to put into words what Gary taught me and did for me? However, once I sat down and started thinking back to the times we met and had lunch, it became very simple and clear for me.

"One of the many things I can certainly say he taught me was the importance of helping others and giving back and especially never forgetting where you came from. At the time, I was working at the Rosen Centre trying to work my way up through the front office, yet here he was, a CEO of Visit Orlando, one of the most important jobs in the state of Florida, someone with so many years of experience, yet he was willing to take the time to help me.

"I can guarantee you won't find many other people willing to do that let alone someone in as high of a position as him. He didn't just write an occasional email, he took the time out of his day to have lunch with me. Every couple of months we would catch up over lunch and just talk, nothing specific, just wherever the conversation would go.

"Another important thing he taught me was about loyalty. I used to think that loyalty was about you doing anything and everything for someone else, or that company. You may not want to do it or agree with the way something had to be done but you were 'loyal' because at any given time, no matter what, when or where, you would be counted on to get the job done or be there for that someone or something. And, in some aspects, that is what loyalty is about, but it's not a one-way street.

"Another time Gary told me, 'It sounds like you have tried to do everything possible and shown your loyalty yet where have they shown their loyalty to you?' If someone isn't willing to tell you their plans for you or what they are possibly thinking for your future and try to help you get there, and you have done everything they have asked of you, then you don't have to be loyal back. It's okay to say I'm going to leave this company or try something new, go on a different path.

"The only thing we had in common was that we graduated from the same college, Davis & Elkins College in a very small town in West Virginia. Yet, only having that in common, Gary still took the time to be my mentor. It's hard to describe what a mentor is, but it's much easier to describe what a mentor isn't. A mentor can mean and be so many different things all in one. A true mentor isn't someone you just reach out to when you only need help or a job, a mentor isn't a relationship to take lightly because that person is going out of their way to help you. A great mentor is rare and that relationship is special. It's someone that you can reach out to get unbiased feedback and who's going to be completely honest with you. That's something that I still remember to this day, when he told me that his feedback may not be what I want to hear but he will be honest with me and give his thoughts. HONESTY. You must both be honest with each other and that's why he or she is your mentor. It's someone whom you can talk to and not worry about if he or she is going to go and tell your boss or laugh at you for asking questions you wouldn't normally ask. You have to accept that the feedback given may not be what you want to hear, however, it is with the best of intentions and coming from a good place.

"The last time we met was in his office. I still remember the first time I walked into it. I was overwhelmed with how amazing it was. I thought to myself, 'I am in way over my head meeting him.' Gary couldn't have been any nicer or more welcoming the first time we met. But the last time we met, two things specifically stood out for me and the irony in them is very scary for me as just a week or two after we met, he passed away. First, he said that life will throw you curveballs; you just need to learn how to deal with them and hit them. Well, Gary's passing was the biggest curveball I've had to deal with in my life, but I hope what I've done in my life so far he would be proud of. Second, we discussed my future and he said that he would get me to the door, but I had to get myself through it, and if I did, then it would be because of me, not him.

"That's another thing he taught me about mentorship – a mentor doesn't get you the job. Your mentor helps you along the way to get the job, but it's you who ultimately must not only open the door but step through it."

Continuing education is one of the most important endeavors you can pursue for yourself. Be a knowledgeable worker. Whether it's the attainment of a master's degree, an increased proficiency in technology, a foreign language, additional learning on a subject matter or industry certification, continuing education reinforces your credentials. It helps you stand out from the crowd. Expanding educational interests can also open up additional opportunities. It's a wonderful way to extend your personal brand with credibility.

A Few Questions to Ask Yourself

- What are you doing/planning to increase your educational portfolio?
- Are you attending/continuing education sessions to improve any area of need?
- Are customers asking for insight you wish you had?
- Have you studied your role models? What educational attributes do they have that you may not have?

- Have you studied your competitors – not the company brand but the individual(s) – with whom you compete?

- Are they more successful? If so, why? What part of your educational portfolio is missing?

No matter what background each of us possesses, **we can learn something new tomorrow**. Additionally, we can strengthen our educational portfolio in the areas we have deficiencies. The mission is to honestly admit to yourself you do not need to know everything! That's okay. The benefit is doing something about it. Building your educational repertoire will foster your presence within your senior management, your peers and your customers.

Insight is the most sought-after credential. Insight is a combination of education, experience and professional curiosity. The ability of your personal brand to be perceived as the "one in the know" is extremely powerful. Think about the most effective hotel concierges. They are personal brands. Guests stay with their hotels in a large part due to the personal attention and insight they provide their guests. Whether it's the newest restaurant in town, the hottest nightclub or the closest coffee house, concierges live and die by their personal recommendations. They must have the insight to back them up.

IBRAND is based on experiences. We are only believable if we have been there, done it! Think of a travel agent. What they truly offer is insight through personal experiences. How do you recommend a cruise if you have never cruised? How do you sell Hawaii if you have never been? How do you recommend a 5-star resort if you have never stayed? The credibility of your personal brand is the insight you offer that cannot be duplicated by anyone else.

This is an interview Olivia Sain had with **Lisa Reed**, the Director of the Office of Career Services & Employment at Davis & Elkins College. It was conducted to show Millennials – from a career development perspective – how personal branding can impact success.

1) **Are you seeing a trend in today's students? Positive or negative?**

I see both. Today's students don't seem to possess the ability to feel comfortable communicating. It's not that they can't do it – I sometimes think they are too afraid to have face-to-face communication with a stranger because they've become so accustomed to texting or hiding behind social media. I almost see a look of terror in their eyes at the thought of networking when I discuss it in class. Your father gave them one of the best pieces of advice when he spoke to a class via Skype in 2012 – he told them to learn to speak in public because it can be such a boost to their confidence in many other facets of life. The No. 1 trait that employers are looking for is the ability to communicate effectively. They somehow have to get past this hurdle, whatever it takes. I used to hold a networking event on campus with employers, alumni and students. It created a safe environment for students to learn the art of working a room. Practice makes perfect, and the more you do it, the easier it'll get.

The positive out of this that I see is that students are also using their technical abilities to sell themselves to prospective employers who could use some help with their online presence. I don't think students always realize that what they do on a daily basis online can be a real selling point to an organization – but I always tell them to use it to their advantage (especially with our local, smaller employers). I see the light bulb come on for them when they discover another selling point they have in their arsenal.

Another positive about our students is that because they have accepted the ideas of diversity and non-traditional (in fact, some of them seem to run from anything traditional), they tend to be a little more open-minded when it comes to a career. Many of ours are willing to relocate, work odd hours or weekends, or think outside of the box when it comes to the functions of their career. I love a student with a "whatever it takes" attitude about their career. Those students will go places.

2) **What qualities do you hope to see more of in your students?**
Enthusiasm and an inquisitive mind. Getting excited about something, researching it in-depth to learn everything you can about it, then going full steam ahead in order to obtain it is what propels you to the next level in life. Students who have no motivation and no direction are the hardest for me to work with and, obviously, the hardest to employ. I give them the tools necessary to find their direction – it's up to them to use what they've learned.

3) **What frustrates you the most about the students?**
Failing to follow through, unprofessional communication and failing to proofread their work.

4) **Is there a deteriorating quality or skill in today's students?**
In addition to my opinion about the role texting has

played on students' inability to communicate, I feel that social media and helicopter parents have played a big role in deteriorating skills in students. Students, please don't think that employers want to know every dirty detail of your life. Yes, they'll check your Facebook, Twitter and Instagram accounts and would probably like to hire someone who doesn't tell the world about their latest breakup, who they slept with last night, how much they drank, or how stressed they are (child, you don't even KNOW what stress is yet!). That's what branding is all about – portraying yourself as someone that employers will fight to employ. So one piece of advice that I tell my own kids as well as college students is "keep your junk in the trunk." As for helicopter parents .... ugh .... please let your kids grow up!! Life skills are lacking in general, I feel. This is exacerbated by parents who hover and do everything for their children and don't allow them to figure things out for themselves, experience failure, and generally guide them through life by the hand. Another one of my favorite phrases I use daily is "figure it out" and I leave it at that. Figuring things out for yourself at a young age will help build independence and give you a sense of accomplishment and pride to help boost confidence.

5) **What unrealistic expectations does the younger generation have when applying for a job?**
That's easy – they think the job will come looking for them and they'll get paid big bucks. What I see often is that students don't realize that their job search begins in their freshman year. Seriously. Building the resume, researching their chosen career field (or multiple career fields if they haven't decided yet), informational

interviews (this is what our students did with your dad via Skype), being proactive in getting multiple internships, building relationships with people who can help in their career search down the road – these are all essential parts of walking off campus and into a job. Finding a job is a full-time job! The other thing would be doing some research on what they can expect to be paid. A little research (or even calling employers to inquire what a typical starting pay looks like) will help them to be more realistic when negotiating compensation and planning a budget. Also, there is no shame in starting at the bottom and being the one who has to make sure there is always fresh coffee in the break room. A good manager knows the duties of every job up the ladder, usually because he/she has done them all.

6) **What's your advice for students entering the workplace?**
Research *yourself* before you go a step further into college. If you don't know who you are, what makes you tick, what you're good at, what you can offer, or what you're passionate about, then you may be choosing the wrong career path. Don't make decisions based on what's "hot" at the moment or what you see on TV – that's not reality. Your ideal job combines your passion with what you're good at. Don't choose a career that doesn't get you excited every day to get out of bed and go to it.

7) **In what areas are college students lacking to get their desired job after graduation?**
In some ways, drive and determination are lacking. Ask questions (lots of questions) to people who work

in that industry, find a mentor, shadow someone on the job, volunteer for your dream company, join an association and go to their annual conference, stay up on current trends in the market and meet key players in the market, meet the people that work in that industry and don't just meet them, bond with them. If you do these things, a student can find that several things may happen: You'll find out who is hiring before it is formally announced, a company you volunteer/intern at may create a position for you because you've proven your ambition, and you'll be far ahead of your classmates.

8) **Is personal branding relevant to your students? Is it even on their radar?**

I do discuss the term "branding," but I would guess I'm the only one on campus who puts much emphasis on it. Personal branding is something that I preach a lot about, but I probably don't use the term as much as I should. I think that our marketing students "get it," more because it's a common term for them, but other students are most likely unfamiliar with the idea.

9) **How would you rate your students' style (attitude, presentation, etiquette?)**

My guess is that they are average with other college students. I do have several very polished and ambitious students, and the interesting thing that I notice is that they seem to come from two distinct backgrounds: those who give credit to their parents for teaching them how to present themselves and those who have been totally supporting themselves. Most of the others have potential if they take the initiative to learn proper etiquette and protocol.

10) How important is mentoring to your students?

I really stress the importance of finding a mentor to our students. I, myself, have a mentor even at my age. For any student who is interested in finding someone to mentor them, I am willing to go to great lengths to find them someone who will be a great teacher to them. I am disappointed to say that very few students take the steps to find a mentor. People in higher education, as well as those who are willing to mentor students, do not do what we do for ourselves. We do it because we love doing it and many of us have a calling for this line of service. However, too often I notice that students don't take the time to properly thank those who have helped them along the way. So often I see students waltz off campus after graduation without thanking their professors, their advisors, their mentors for helping them to learn, grow and become successful. Students, please remember, a heartfelt "thank you" is what makes our jobs worthwhile. Be gracious and thankful.

Lisa Reed continues about her connection with Gary.

❝As the Director of the Office of Career Services & Student Employment at Gary's alma mater, Davis & Elkins College in Elkins, W.Va., it is my goal to build a network of alumni who are passionate about giving back to their college, mentoring, and opening doors for our students. I have had the great pleasure of working with many such alumni but, by far, one of the most influential people I have worked with thus far was Gary Sain. I was introduced to him through a member of the college's National Alumni Council, but I had already heard of Gary's professional career and knew he was someone I needed on my side.

"Usually when I work with a professional of Gary's degree, I am accustomed to working around their schedule and patiently waiting for a return phone call or email. Gary was different. He returned my calls and emails within hours, not days or weeks. He was eager to help. He got his staff involved working with me as well. His first presentation to our students took the form of a Skype informational interview for one of Chef Melanie Campbell's hospitality classes. Each student was required to stand and ask Gary a career-related question. I was amazed at the ease with which he spoke, how polished he was, and how relevant his answers were to where these students were in their lives. I think we were all mesmerized by him (I know I was). My favorite words of advice from him were, 'Learn how to speak in public – you'll never regret it.'

"In April 2012, the Davis & Elkins Hospitality Club traveled to Orlando. My part in this trip was to organize the educational component of the trip and, as usual, Gary was eager to help. He arranged for our students to visit the 2012 NPE International Plastics Showcase. After many years of holding their expo in Chicago, this was the first year they switched their venue to Orlando, and this was of great pride to Gary and a boost to the Orlando economy. Gary arranged for a tour of the expo and a private room to meet our students in. Until that point, my conversations with Gary were all on the phone. However, the first thing he did when he walked in the room was come straight to me and give me a big hug and thanked me for the chance to meet our students – it was like meeting a long-lost friend for the first time. I think the students were in awe to have someone of Gary's magnitude take time from his busy day to spend it with them, and several of them saw the value in what Gary could offer and kept in touch via email after we left Orlando. I always teach students that when you find a connection like Gary, you do NOT let it go. "

chapter 6

Standards
(How You Do It)

Another day I'll never forget was Oct. 3, 1995. It started off as hectic, but not unusual. I remember rushing to get Olivia downtown to be tested for special education services in the public school system. Gary had rushed out the door that morning because he had a long day ahead of him. I knew he would call throughout the day to check on us and to see how our day was going. It was his habit since he spent so much time on the road. He was always just a phone call away from the girls and me.

We had just arrived at the appointment. As we walked into the reception room, we noticed that all eyes were glued to the television set. It was the day the O.J. Simpson verdict was expected. Gary had already called a few times to hear if there was any news. He had just left an appointment with AAA and was heading back to Cape Canaveral.

In what seemed like only a few minutes, my phone rang again. It was Gary. In a shaky voice he immediately said, *"I'm okay."* He had just been in a car accident. All of a sudden the television reporters broke from the trial and showed scenes of the wreck. It was on the Bee Line – a stretch of highways from Orlando to the coast known as "donor alley." It was nicknamed that due to all the fatal crashes.

As he was driving, Gary had tried to answer his cell phone but it fell to the floor. He reached down to retrieve it and a flatbed semi pulled out in front of him. As he straightened up and noticed the truck, he over-corrected and lost control of his car. He veered in front of the semi, rolled into the brush on the side of the road and hit a tree. His car was upended and landed on the driver's side completely totaled.

Somehow, Gary had gotten himself out of the car and was standing on the side of the road when the paramedics and fire trucks arrived. One of the emergency workers told Gary that the poor guy in the smashed car couldn't have made it out alive. Gary said, "I'm the guy!"

Pretty shaken up and worried about Gary, I told him we were leaving immediately to come get him. He assured me he would be fine. He then explained to me that the colleague who had been following behind in his own car would take him to work. He was going to have to let one of his team members go that day and it was not right to have someone else do that. It was his responsibility and he would see it through. Having just walked away from a near-fatal car accident, he could very well have chosen to take the rest of the day off and let someone else handle the firing. But that's not who Gary was. He was all about accountability!

That night, I told him that surely his guardian angel had watched over him and we had all escaped something terrible. I told him his job was not yet done here on Earth. I felt reassured at that moment that Gary was meant for greater things.

In Gary's Words:
Standards are how you do what you do. They are your personal

benchmarks or individual commitments you make to yourself. They are your code of individual performance. The higher your mark, the more distinctive your personal brand will become.

Standards of your personal brand should be well thought out and written down. If it is not in writing, it does not exist. Think about your position within your company, your involvement within your community, your family, etc. How do you want to perform your duties and responsibilities? What do you think is acceptable or not acceptable? More importantly, how do you want to create a personal distinction within your work, community and family through your actions? What are your ethical standards? Selling standards? Leadership standards? Customer service standards?

Think about the customers you serve. They have choices. Set high customer service standards. Develop ways to make your customers more profitable. Do what you said you were going to do, when you said you were going to do it, and how you said you were going to do it. Personal customer standards help to ensure you are delivering excellence to your targeted audience. By the way, excellence is not optional for **iBRAND**.

'Clear Expectations'
The way Gary did anything was the epitome of high-standard **iBRAND**ing. His word was always gold, even if it meant spending time overseeing the most minute details...because it meant leaving his personal mark on any project.

Beth Ann Carr, President of INSPIRI Consulting, was amazed that Gary personally signed 450 silent auction requests for a United Way campaign despite his busy schedule...because he said he would.

"I first met Gary in 2007 while working for Heart of Florida United Way. Gary was asked to chair the hospitality division of our Campaign Committee, which was composed of community leaders who volunteer to help United Way generate and meet the financial goals during the annual campaign. I must admit, I was a bit nervous about our first meeting. Gary's reputation of excellence had preceded him, and because of his role in the community, I wanted to be sure we could work well together and succeed. The energy I spent on nerves, I would learn, was completely wasted.

"To my relief, Gary was as welcoming and friendly as if I'd known him for many years. This, I would soon learn, was not unique to my specific experience, but was authentic to Gary's style. His easy likability and positive manner is how he was with everyone; authentically interested in others, unpretentious, honest, kind, and an expert at putting anyone at ease. His charisma was infectious yet unassuming and drew everyone into the positive energy that he emitted as easily as anyone breathes. Bottom line is that if you weren't at ease around Gary, there was something wrong with you.

"As we strategized about the upcoming campaign, Gary was upfront about the demands of his schedule, yet insisted that we not limit what we do, only manage how and when we do it. If he was anyone else, I might have been suspect as to how this would work, but again, with Gary, his authentic and genuine manner left me no room to doubt.

"Although Gary was not expected to assist with any of the manual labor of the campaign except encouraging the hospitality industry to run employee workplace campaigns, he offered to help with the silent auction of the Annual Chef's Gala. We generated a list of people to contact for auction gifts, and he agreed to sign each letter personally. When the list was finalized, I remembered Gary's earlier statement about his schedule demands and believed I would most definitely need to purge the list. It wasn't short. It contained more than 450 companies we intended to make a request of. The easy thing would be to have an electronic signature printed on every letter.

"When I let Gary know how long the list was, I was certain we would use an electronic signature. However, he said, 'No electronic signature, I want to sign them personally, so if you can get them to me by Friday, I'll sign them over the weekend before I leave on Monday.' I was both surprised and again not so surprised; as Gary had proven many times, he would do what he said he would do. With his standards of excellence and his character I knew he would do his part. We got the letters to him on a Friday. Not only did Gary hand sign each of the 450 letters, he wrote a quick personal note on each one!

"I have to say, Gary inspired many people around him, and they were willing to do whatever they could to support him. He always went above and beyond, and you never felt you owed him for it. He was the kind of person you wanted to know, and learn from. Once Gary's cabinet term was over, I would run into him at social and community events. He was always pleased to see you and always had time for a chat.

"Gary never met a stranger, welcomed everyone and will be greatly missed for his kind and generous nature. His standards of excellence, his warm style made him beloved by everyone in our community. The impact of his successes and ability to bring people together to make our community a better place to live continues to this day and will for a long time to come.

"It was a great privilege to know Gary and to work with him even for a short time. What a wonderful world this would be if more people were like him."

Your standards significantly influence how others perceive you. If you want to be perceived as an individual who is committed to doing a great job, what are your quality standards? The same holds true for community involvement. If you want people to perceive you as a "can do" person, what are your networking standards? And it holds true with your family. If you want people to perceive you as a strong family person, what are your relationship standards with your spouse, children, etc.?

Some Questions to Consider

- What are my personal standards for customer interaction (i.e., returning phone calls)?

- What are my leadership standards (i.e., spending quality time with staff)?

- What are my personal standards for meetings (i.e., showing up on time)?

- Do I have zero tolerance for errors in my work (i.e., letters, correspondence, etc.)?

- What are my sales standards (i.e., make one new sales contact per day)?

- What are my customer service standards (i.e., resolving problems on the spot)?

- Do I inspect what I expect (i.e., don't assume)?

- Am I committed to excellence in everything I do? How do I measure?

- What are my family standards (i.e., quality time per week)?

- Am I trustworthy in everything I do? Do I check with myself?

- Is my word my bond? Do I have it written down? Do I hold myself accountable?

Standards bring credibility and respectability to your personal brand through actions. Actions are what shape human beings. Standards support the brand you want to be. Standards are the criteria that ensure your personal brand is delivering your brand promise. Think of a brand standards manual for a company. Why should your personal brand be any less important? Put it in writing and it will become more tangible and real.

Think about the brand you purchase from each and every day. If they don't deliver on the brand promise, you eventually move on to another competitor. The same is true for your personal brand. If you don't deliver the report on time, properly take care of your customers, or produce the desired results expected of you, your superior, customer or peer may lose confidence in your ability and performance. Worse, they may bypass you altogether.

Doing what you said you were going to do, when you said you were going to do it, and how you said you were going to do it is your brand promise! They are the actions that help create your perception with your targeted audience.

Personal brand standard development is at the sole discretion of the individual. Granted, your current job has standards that must be met. However, your personal brand standards are customized to fit your individual brand. Yes, they reinforce how you do your current job. More importantly, they are helping to support you for your next position, as well as your overall career. You must first review where you are today and where you want to go!

Mapping out a personal LifePlan to reach your desired goal(s) will shed light on what personal standards you wish to embrace in support of your overall objectives. Many of us don't have a personal LifePlan for ourselves, or at least not written down. We should. It helps to commit to writing what we want to do with our lives and where we want to end up.

Gary would often share his thoughts about pursuing one's passion. **Karen Soto**, Vice President of Human Resources with Visit Orlando, noticed that his approach to life and career taught others how to seize the day.

> "Gary talked about how you need to do what's in your heart. If you're not passionate about what you do every day, then you shouldn't be doing it. Life is too short. We could see it in Gary's eyes that he was truly passionate about what he did and wanted every team member to be just as passionate about what they were doing every day, and if they weren't, they needed to find a journey and a path to get there."

Taking into consideration the individual (internal or external) with whom you are competing with for future opportunities can also add insight to your personal LifePlan. It will help frame strengths and weaknesses. In addition, having a mentor can help ensure your personal standards are achieving the desired results. Your mentor can also help you judge if your personal brand standards are in support of your goals. This is critical. Everyone needs an objective third party for guidance and honest feedback.

Bottom line: Your personal brand standards are the glue that reinforces your LifePlan and ensures you can deliver on your personal brand promise!

Here are three topic categories for personal brand standards. I believe these are most pertinent to many of us. However, **i**BRAND is all about you and is totally personalized. You may wish to add additional topic categories. My critical three topic categories are:

- Leadership by Example
- Under-Promise, Over-Deliver
- Creative Problem-Solving

Leadership by Example

Leadership is not solely based on title or responsibilities. Everyone can lead by example regardless of position, accountabilities or affiliation. For those of us who have families, we know this principle all too well. Children measure you for what you do, not what you say. It's no different in the workforce. To build respect, confidence and trust, **let actions speak louder than words!** The standards you choose to support your daily performance will provide you a framework to work within, and more importantly, help to hold you accountable.

Gary definitely walked the walk when it came to leading by example. **Steve Joyce**, President & CEO, Choice Hotels International (as featured on *Undercover Boss*), watched how Gary humbly worked with others, stepping aside to watch them succeed.

"Gary Sain epitomized everything that was good about the meetings travel industry. A poster child for success, he started at the bottom and, through hard work, a commanding work ethic and unwavering confidence, rose through the ranks to become the President and CEO of one of the nation's top convention centers and DMOs in the country.

"First and foremost, everything Gary did was with a thoughtful mind and a humble heart. He grew people and their talents. He believed in them, many times opening their eyes to the possibilities and a future that might have once been a foregone conclusion. Outlooks were changed, attitudes adjusted and new approaches embraced, all while remaining authentic to what he embodied and how he lived his life. He preached through action: a 'do as I do' and 'believe in yourself as I believe in you' kind of mentality.

"Gary advocated that at the core for any amount of success, you need to first believe in yourself and the team who is going to make it happen. His ❙BRAND concept is about the power of 'I' – the power of understanding your strengths and your ability – the power to set things in motion – the power to begin to change the world. Gary was the champion in marshaling forward the concept of extolling your own brand, staying true to who you are and serving as a beacon for others along the way.

"One life can change many, and Gary continues to do in so many ways."

We are all leaders in the way we conduct our lives and manage our careers. We are responsible to ourselves for our daily actions. Sure, we all report to someone. However, you are the one in charge of your personal brand, its performance and its destiny. Taking charge is the first step. That's leadership in itself. Demonstrating your leadership capabilities through actions is the second step. Building a reputation is the third step.

True leaders can leave their mark while transforming lives and communities. **Teresa Jacobs**, Orange County mayor, watched Gary's legacy unfold as his vision propelled Orlando and Orange County, Fla., into a tourist destination that was envied yet respected.

"Great leaders are what our nation and communities are built upon. They are the ones who not only charge ahead, bringing their goals and vision to fruition, but also inspire others to follow suit. They are the visionaries who spark change and bring about innovation, never letting anything or anyone stand in their way. These individuals are the driving force behind moving us forward and making things happen.

"Whether you knew him personally or not, it was clear that Gary Sain had a genuine passion for the Central Florida region and epitomized what made a great leader and industry visionary. His passion, foresight and intellect made Gary a champion, not only for our region, but the entire travel and tourism industry. He took over our tourism bureau in 2007, and as a result of his hard work, Orlando-Orange County was not only the No. 1 destination to visit in 2011, but also recognized as one of the best places to do business.

"Gary's boundless energy and commitment went beyond his love for the tourism industry. He was also dedicated to charitable community organizations, which were second only to his devotion to his wife and two daughters. Gary was an all-around great man and will truly be missed.

"In his eulogy to his father, Gary said, 'We all come into this world ordinary and it's how we live our lives, how we serve those we are responsible for and how we love others that determines if we leave this world extraordinary.' Gary Sain was extraordinary."

The key is to identify the most important personal standards and commit to them. As stated before, these standards should be based on your personal brand. No two individuals are alike. Nor are their standards. Your "leadership by example" standards are those that have the greatest relevance to you. They are what truly separates you from everyone else.

Brad Dean, President & CEO of Visit Myrtle Beach, knows that passion for teamwork and exceptional perception were Gary's iBRAND.

Gary's unique insights and sound judgment enabled him to work collaboratively with people from all walks of life. His passion for the industry and his community were contagious. In so many ways, we could point to Gary as the ideal destination leader. Though he followed in his father's footsteps, Gary effectively distinguished himself with a record of proactive leadership and outstanding accomplishments. He climbed the ladder of success not upon the backs of others, but rather, by their side. And even for those of us who knew him as a competitor, we always found ourselves better simply for knowing this wonderful man.

Again, **if they don't exist in writing, they don't exist at all!** I am a firm believer once you commit your standards in writing, you have a better chance for success. Review them often. No one else needs to evaluate your performance. These are your personal standards to support your brand promise. However, you must hold yourself accountable.

- How do you overcome your largest adversary, the competitor, of indifference?

- How do you make yourself valuable to your stakeholders?

- Do fellow employees come to you for guidance and counsel?

- Are you a mentor? What are your standards for mentorship? What do you look for in a mentor?

- When was the last time you asked your stakeholders to provide feedback on your performance?

- Do you build confidence and trust with your stakeholders?

- Are you a student of your industry trends, competition, niche opportunities? Do you keep abreast of what is going on?

- What are your standards for ensuring you put your best foot forward each and every day? A bad attitude cancels out all positive skills.

- How are you building your image? Who are you associating with to create high-quality associations?

- Are you viewed as a thought leader, change agent or idea person?

- How do you tell your personal brand story in a non-threatening way to communicate your success to your stakeholders?

- Are you a team player? How are you adding more value to your team members?

- Do you insulate yourself with results? Results always speak louder than words. How do you hold yourself accountable?

- Do you treat everyone with dignity and respect, regardless of age, ethnicity, position?

- Whom would you most likely want to emulate? Why?

Under-Promise, Over-Deliver (Delivering 'WOW!')

How you deliver upon the expectations you establish are critical to your future credibility and success. Most of the time, we tend to oversell. We all want to be perceived as competent professionals. However, we sometimes inflate what we think we can deliver or what we think the other person wants to hear. We want to immediately exceed the expectations of our stakeholders. We may be taking a calculated risk, which could backfire on our personal brands reputation if we don't perform up to expectation. A better approach is to always under-promise and over-deliver. I am not advocating you communicate an expectation below the request of your stakeholder. It's more the added value you provide that is not expected.

Doing what is not expected is not only highly memorable, but it creates a distinction for your personal brand. Think about what you do every day. There are numerous opportunities for you to "Kick it up a notch," as Emeril Lagasse would say. It's committing that extra effort that will be the most recognized. It may be as simple as volunteering for a special assignment, adding a value add to a report that was not requested, or rewarding an unsuspecting customer or peer. Granted, you need to fulfill the basic expectation in the mind of your targeted audience in whatever you do. However, if you can add something distinctive, it will be much more recognizable. By the way, it's not the big things that you do; it's the small things that make a difference!

Exceeding the expectations of your stakeholders can create personal brand esteem and distinction. There are plenty of underachievers in the world. Why not stand above the crowd by consistently delivering upon your brand promise by doing it better than anticipated? You need to choose the standards right for you. Put it in writing. Hold yourself accountable each and every day!

- Do you manage your customers/stakeholders' expectations? Do you raise expectations you can't meet?

- Do you surprise and delight? How?

- Do you strive to have work completed prior to due dates?

- Do you send personalized thank-you notes? When was the last time?

- Are you presenting new ideas or concepts to your clients?

- What are your standards for delivering "WOW," the ability to create distinctive experiences with your stakeholders and your personal brand?

- Are you doing the same things this year that you did last year? What are you doing differently?

- Do you ask your stakeholders how you can improve your performance?

- Do you have standards for follow-up (phone, email, appointments, etc.)? Do you have standards for cell phone etiquette?

- How do you ensure you deliver what you said you were going to do and how you said you were going to do it?

Assumptions/unforeseen circumstances can be the kiss of death.

- Do you truly know the individual behind the name of those you interact with the most? Their family, hobbies and what they're passionate about?

Buddy Dyer, mayor of Orlando, learned to expect the unexpected from Gary. To say that he went above and beyond couldn't begin to capture the "WOW" moments.

> The reality of his passing didn't fully register with me until I arrived at work to find a handwritten note from Gary that he had penned just a few days before. Truth be told, the date on the note actually says May 7, three days after he passed away. I'm assuming the note was postdated. But if anyone had the power to continue to work from beyond the grave, it would be Gary! These notes were a common item in my inbox. I looked forward to receiving these simple cards from Gary, which usually included an attachment touting another tourism record being broken in Orlando, pictures of an event or simply notes on a new project Visit Orlando was pursuing. Gary's notes are just one example of the personal touch that made him an incredible ambassador for our community and our tourism industry.
>
> "In the days since his passing, much has been said about the leadership Gary provided to our tourism industry, particularly during the Great Recession. I echo the thoughts of so many in our community in saying that Gary will long be remembered for cementing Orlando as the No. 1 tourism destination in the world."

Creative Problem-Solving

In today's competitive environment, creativity is as important as analytical skills. In fact, the best skill set of the future may very well be a blend of both. I believe creativity in problem solving could be the most important and most underrated. The ability to solve problems or seize new opportunities through creativity will create a discernible difference. The combination of right brain/left brain will be highly sought after. Creativity is not a department. It's not the advertising agency. Creative problem-solving is everyone's job.

Perhaps Gary's ideas were "Insain," but **Roger Dow**, President & CEO of U.S. Travel Association, saw how Gary was always a step ahead in creatively thinking about how to solve a problem.

66Gary was a rare leader with lots of ideas, affectionately known as 'Insane Sain.' He would call me weekly with new ideas for the industry. He was always firing on all cylinders and it was never a moment's rest when it came to exercising his creativity and how to improve upon something. The [flickering] of his energy propelled him forward with thoughts and ideas.

"What set him apart is that he was 'insainly' committed to the ideas and bringing them to fruition with passion and energy. His personality attracted others to share and believe in his ideas with him. To him, nothing was impossible. As long as you put your mind to it, anything is possible.

"He was very proactive in the meetings and exhibitions space. When the meetings industry came under attack, Gary was at the forefront and helped spearhead a campaign that raised $1 million in the span of 12 months to counter the negative rhetoric and go on the offensive to tout the value and importance of meetings – government, business and leisure. 🙶

Creativity can be unleashed with stimulation. Increase your creativity problem-solving skills by taking an art or photography class. Try music lessons or a sculpture class. When was the last time you visited a museum, art show or design expo? What about gourmet cooking or wine seminars? Have you thought about learning another language? Golf can increase focusing skills and identify new approaches. The key is to channel your thinking into new ways of looking at things.

- How do you jump-start your creative juices? What are your passions in life? How do you use them to creatively motivate you?

- Do peers come to you for help in solving their work problems? Do you encourage it? Do you add value to your customers' business? How? When was the last time you brought a new idea to him/her?

- How well do you listen? What are your standards for listening?

- Do you typically ask for several opinions on a business issue or do you tend to gravitate to your line of thinking? Or the easiest solution?

- How much time do you spend in creative thinking? Do you contemplate how to do things better or how to solve problems more creatively?

- Do you ask more questions than you answer?

- Do you tend to offer the first solution that comes to mind or do you creatively come up with new ideas?

- Do you gravitate to new products? Do you buy and use them? What do you learn from using them?

- Are you an optimist or pessimist? When people come to you with new ideas, what is your reaction? Do you encourage or discourage?

- How do you instill creativity within your work environment? How do you keep it fresh?

- Do you have a diverse group of friends? Age? Sex? Ethnicity? Interests?

- Have you participated in a blog, RSS feeds or podcasts?

Standards are the glue that reinforces who you are and what you stand for. The uniqueness of **IBRAND** is that you do it for yourself. True satisfaction and fulfillment in life are best achieved through personal discovery and achievement. **Always be the best you can be!**

chapter 7

Style
(Doing It Your Way)

*The text in this chapter is taken completely from Gary's
published articles, except for quotes from three colleagues
and each anecdote's preceding paragraph.*

Style is doing it your way. Style is your personal trademark. A
trademark unduplicated by any other human being. Style may be
the most memorable core pillar of **iBRAND**. It can also be the
quickest way to end a promising client relationship, business
deal or promotion. Style is how you relate to others. Personal
branding is about emotional connections. Style connects you to
your desired audience [in] a highly distinctive manner.

What are the elements of style? I feel the most important [ones]
in business are **presentation, etiquette** and **attitude**.

pre·sen·ta·tion – *How you dress, how you groom
yourself.*

Presentation is the way you present yourself through visual and
verbal communication to your targeted audience. Presentation
skills make you credible. First impressions are lasting impressions.
Make certain you always put your best foot forward. In addition,

you must manage your personal brand presentation at all times. You may be off the clock, [but] your personal brand is always on display. Best keep your guard up.

- Do people ever compliment you on your appearance?

- When was the last time you updated your wardrobe?

- How about your hairstyle? Are your shoes shined?

- Are you committed to making your appearance the best it can be?

- When was the last time you had someone critique your presentation/verbal skills?

- Do you try to meet new people at a social function? Do you remember their names?

- Are you a good public speaker? Do you work at being better?

- Are you memorable? How?

- Are you a good listener? How?

Nice Guys Finish Brilliantly

First impressions can be game changing. **Simon T. Bailey,** author of *Shift Your Brilliance,* and leader of the Brilliance Movement, recalls an impeccably dressed featured speaker Gary Sain. The most lasting memory etched in Simon's mind is Gary's own level of **i**BRANDing and his ability to creatively influence.

"I first met Gary Sain in 1990 when I went to work for Hyatt Regency Atlanta Airport. I was invited to participate in a national sales meeting and he was one of the featured speakers. As he approached the podium to share his latest thinking, the first thing I noticed was his custom-made

Italian suit, custom monogrammed cuff link shirt, Brioni tie, and spit-shined Salvatore Ferragamo shoes. Major advertising firms state that people size you up in three to seven seconds. Well, if this is true, I decided in that instant moment that Gary Sain was a first-class act, wicked-smart as they would say in Boston, and authentically nice.

"Experts say that leadership is both caught and taught. It was that day and that moment I saw what it meant to look brilliant and think brilliant. There was a spark lit in me to always look my best, no matter what was happening. Gary painted an image on the canvas of my consciousness with his energetic spirit and contagious charisma.

"As I grew in my career at Hyatt Hotels & Resorts, I continued to witness Gary's marketing genius at work. He was a force of nature and would never, ever settle for status quo living or an average existence. As time passed, our careers went in divergent directions. We bumped into each other 10 years later at a Mother's Day brunch at the Hyatt Regency Grand Cypress. At that time he was the CMO for the Big Red Boat. We didn't know that we were both living in Florida. We exchanged business cards and agreed to stay in touch. Well, through the busyness of life, we lost contact until I was asked by Peter Yesawich in 2004 to join him at Y Partnership as senior vice president of diversity marketing, and little did I know that I would have the privilege of reuniting with Gary Sain.

"We were both excited to be working with Peter, who is revered as a travel industry icon. However, it was in the moments when I would pop into Gary's office that he would share with me his latest thinking on branding. It was there where I first began to hear him talk about the power of a smile. As you may know, this would eventually become the award-winning marketing campaign for Visit Orlando that further cemented Gary's marketing genius in the travel industry. Yes, it's true, I would happen to be in the office and wander by his office and he would say, 'Let me run something by you,' and in that instant I became a focus group of one. Gary was brilliant! Off-the-chart creative and always thinking about the future."

---

et·i·quette – *How you treat people, how you value what's important to them and how you place others before yourself.*

Etiquette is defined as the rules and customs for polite, social or professional behavior. Etiquette skills provide a proper framework for you to interact with people. Since we live and interact in a diverse society, it is paramount that your personal brand positioning is sensitive to the cultural, political and religious fabric of your targeted audience. I would encourage you not to judge a book by its cover. Many embarrassing moments have occurred with quick assessments of people that may not have been correct.

- Do you manage your cell phone with regard to those around you?
- Do you totally focus on the person you are speaking to?
- Are you sensitive to other people's beliefs and denominations?
- Are you sensitive to other people's time?
- Do you properly introduce people?
- Do you remember to properly thank people?

- Do you interrupt people?

- Do you label people unfairly?

- Are you knowledgeable about other customs?

- Are you geo-savvy, meaning do you understand world geography?

Gary exuded an unequaled intuitiveness that won over anyone who was lucky enough to know him. His passion for both people and whatever he set his mind to wasn't lost on **Mark McHugh**, President & CEO of Gatorland.

"I first met Gary during the executive search to find a new CEO for the Orlando/Orange County Convention & Visitors Bureau, which later became Visit Orlando through Gary's vision and branding leadership. I was chairman of the search committee and Gary had contacted me with interest in the job. Having never met Gary, I arranged for a breakfast meeting along with Jim Atchison from Sea World, who had known Gary for quite some time. Gary had no 'C-level' experience, but had enjoyed a very successful career in the sales and marketing arena.

"During the breakfast meeting, Gary was trying to feel us out to see if this was really something he wanted to do, because at the time he seemed comfortable in his job at a large advertising and public relations firm. He seemed nervous during the meeting and would interrupt Jim and me to ask questions before we had time to finish answering the previous question, and I thought at the time, 'Man, this guy doesn't listen very well.' This initial thought turned out to be the furthest from the truth. Through subsequent meetings and interviews, I saw a guy with genuine warmth, strength and passion for people and tourism marketing. The selection committee chose Gary over several CEOs from the nation's top destination marketing organizations, bringing a relative unknown to the CVB world to lead one of the country's premier sales and marketing organizations: a pretty bold move at the time.

"I was fortunate to be chairman of the board for Visit Orlando during Gary's first two years as CEO. I immediately found Gary to be completely opposite of my initial impression from our first breakfast meeting. Gary was a great 'listener.' Whether you met him accidentally in a restaurant or on the floor of one of the country's largest trade shows, he'd make you feel like there was no one else in the world more important to him at that moment than you. He seemed to block out the bustle of all the activities around him and focus intently on your conversation. With that huge smile and his eyes focused right on you, there was no doubt that you had his complete attention, and the conversation did not end until your concerns were discussed. He left no doubt that he cared about you, your issues and your thoughts.

"I was able to tell Gary on a couple of occasions how rewarding it was for me to watch him grow as a CEO and become one of the finest leaders in our industry. He had a quiet confidence that was overshadowed by his humility, a very rare characteristic in CEOs. We took a chance when we hired someone without DMO experience, but he made us look brilliant.

"A brand is a very complex topic. It is far more than just an image or slogan. A brand is the bond you create with those around you, and the belief they have in your ability to deliver on the promises you make. You must be consistent in your messages, your priorities, and your ethics. Gary thoroughly understood this when it came to leadership and how you live your life. He lived consistently true to his message.

"As a great leader, Gary focused equally on the lives of everyone in a 360-degree circle around him, and not just the thoughts or wishes of his bosses. He was concerned with the lives of all his employees, his peers in the industry, his board of directors and especially his family. It seemed to me at times that Gary was driven more by a fear of failure than a thirst for success. The thought that he might do something that would disappoint his employees, his friends or his family drove him to be true in his thoughts, his words and his actions. You can interview a hundred people who knew Gary, from casually to very well, and they would all use these words and phrases to describe him. Now *that* is great iBRAND! Gary lived up to his brand promise each and every day."

***

at·ti·tude – *Your mindset, your passion, your enthusiasm for what you do.*

Attitude drives actions. Actions drive results. Results drive lifestyle. What lifestyle you want for yourself and your family will determine your attitude. Attitude determines if you will maximize your full personal brand potential, thereby achieving your personal goals. A negative attitude cancels out all positive skills. Indifference is deadly. Attitude determines how you approach each and every day – whether your glass is half full or half empty.

Are you passionate about what you do? How?

- Are you excited about your future?

- Is your enthusiasm contagious? Do people like being around you?

- Are you energetic? Do you smile often?

- Do you relish coming to your job each and every day? If not, why?

- Are you respectful to everyone you interact with?

- Are you a "can do" person? Do you demonstrate it?

- Do you use humor to connect with people?

- Is your attitude a "me" attitude or a "we" attitude?

- Do you make it right each and every time? How?

- Do you believe in yourself? What about others?

Half full or half empty? **Paul Mears**, Hello! Destination Management & Mears Transportation Group, worked side-by-side with Gary for years. The one thing that he remembers most is that Gary always kept it positive, no matter the obstacles.

"My time with Gary was inspirational. It wasn't an incident, it was the everyday approach to all personal engagement that impacted me. As a member of Visit Orlando's Board of Directors and the incoming Chairman during Gary's tenure, I interacted with him for several years on a wide variety of topics and all types of situations – organizational strategy and board approval, personnel decisions, political realities, client opportunities and conflict, and more. I watched Gary engage in a crowd, at podiums, in a boardroom and in back rooms with a small group of people or just me. His positive disposition never changed. That is not to say he was always happy with the results. Gary was a serious man with high ambition who encountered real obstacles. He didn't see the world through rose-colored glasses. But his approach was always positive. Even when the path he advocated was under attack, he kept listening, engaged, respectful and positive. His belief that there was a good outcome was unshakable and it influenced those around him to get to that positive result.

"Gary's approach is always on my mind. His way of constant but genuine positivity serves as my benchmark. I cannot reproduce it, but I believe he changed the way I work for the better, and I am grateful."

Your credentials, standards and style help convey your personal brand story. How you are being positioned by your boss, your customers or your peers is based on how your personal brand story is being told. This is the reason word-of-mouth advertising is so critical in branding. Recommendations by friends, family and associates are the most credible forms of information sources used in making purchasing decisions, especially travel. This is no different than your personal brand. Your personal brand story will be told regardless of whether you want it told or not. I would suggest you manage it diligently so the right story is being told.

My hope is to motivate you to think differently about yourself. Today is the first day of the rest of your life. It means that every day is a new beginning. As sales and marketing professionals, we spend a great deal of time ensuring the brand we work for is well positioned in the marketplace. We should spend more time on the most important brand in the world – ourselves!

One last quote, which I have always liked, is "If you are not the lead dog, the view always looks the same." As basic as it sounds, it has incredible merit. In order to stand out from the crowd, you need to execute your personal brand plan to create a distinction for yourself. It's up to you. The view is much better if it is your own!

chapter 8

The 'InSain' Challenge

The "InSain" Challenge was a work in progress throughout Gary's career. His job required him to be in top physical shape in order to keep up with the rigor of travel. He was a firm believer that you needed to take care of your body, from the inside and out. Fast forward, and along came the initiative of the "InSain" Challenge at Visit Orlando.

Gary was big on walking. He wore a pedometer to make sure he exceeded 10,000 steps a day. It was never unusual to find him on his cell phone, at the office, walking around the building, encouraging his team to put on their walking shoes to join him for a lap or two to chat.

In December 2010, Gary had a full hip replacement. His goal was to be back at work by the second week of January...not using a cane! Well, I can tell you it was not 10 days after his surgery before he was doing laps around the neighborhood in his walker. He later graduated to laps at the mall. He was relentless. I truly believe his dedication to exercise helped mold him into a strong, disciplined leader.

Here is the original email Gary sent to community leaders requesting them to join him in the "InSain" Challenge:

"Join me in the InSain Orlando Executive Challenge. Together with our leaders I'm convinced we can send an important message to our circle of friends, employees and the entire community. Bolder Media Group has become nationally syndicated on PBS radio and television and whose presence on the Internet has grown to attract a huge audience interested in how fitness (physical and mental) can make our lives longer and healthier.

"I'm asking that you step out beyond your normal routine to do something really different to add to your fitness routine and let the folks from Bolder spend 30 minutes with you to capture your story on video.

"Their Emmy Award-winning team will produce a feature to appear on WUCF-TV and a number of partner websites, including the Orlando Sentinel, WMFE, Growing Bolder, and promoted all over social media networks and through a publicity campaign. There will be a dedicated website for the challenge featuring your video and all of our other friends who are joining in.

"There will be a one-hour TV special featuring all of the participating executives who've stepped up to the challenge, and throughout, we will be focused on driving those you inspired to get active and take the Healthy Central Florida pledge. Please let me know that you are officially 'InSain!'"

'Leading by Example'
With Gary's InSain Challenge, **Marc Middleton**, Founder & CEO

of Bolder Media Group, found himself at the forefront of Gary's health initiative. It's there that he saw firsthand Gary's inspiring commitment and legendary leadership.

"I knew of Gary Sain (everybody did) but never really got to know him until I read that he was doing 1,200 pushups on his 61st birthday to challenge his 175 staff members to make healthy lifestyle choices.

"It was the kind of story I loved to tell, so I reached out to Gary and requested an interview. He invited me into his home and while he did pushups on the living room floor, we chatted about his InSain Challenge. 'It's all about motivating my staff,' he told me. 'If they see me doing this many pushups, maybe they'll be motivated to get more active and commit to a regular fitness routine.'

"The more we talked, the more I realized that it really wasn't insane at all. Gary was well aware that exercise and a healthy diet could translate into more creative, energetic and productive employees and would ultimately reduce company health-care costs. 'But at the same time,' he said, 'It's a tremendous personal benefit to our team members whose lives will be much richer and more active. It's the ultimate win-win, and it all starts with leadership.'

"And that's when the idea clicked. Leadership. More specifically, leading by example. It was one of the many things Gary was known for. I asked if he would be willing to extend his InSain Challenge to other corporate and civic leaders. 'Absolutely,' he answered immediately.

"Gary was renowned for his passion and his work ethic. Upon learning of our project, a mutual friend warned me, 'Be ready for phone calls on weekends and in the middle of the night from a hotel room in Europe. When Gary gets excited about something, he never stops thinking about it.'

"He was right. I had a front-row seat to the tour de force that was Gary Sain and I enjoyed every minute. He was one of the best collaborators I have ever worked with, immensely talented at quickly and efficiently pushing a project forward. Within days, he sent personal letters to a who's who of Central Florida executives, challenging them to share their favorite workout on camera to help inspire not only their employees but also the entire Central Florida community.

"Saying 'no' to Gary wasn't easy. Over the next several months we produced video stories on Harris Rosen, President and COO of Rosen Hotels & Resorts, Simon Hemus, President and COO of Tupperware, Lars Houmann, President and CEO of Florida Hospital, Orlando Mayor Buddy Dyer, Ann Sonntag, Publisher of the Orlando Business Journal, Tony Jenkins, Market President for Florida Blue, and many others. We showed a side of them that very few had ever seen: in swimming pools, hot yoga classes, riding bikes, paddle boarding, lifting weights and much more. They shared not only their private workouts but also their personal feelings about exercise and nutrition.

"It was most definitely not a grassroots effort. It was a top-down effort. It was leading by example and it was definitive Gary Sain. Together we spread the message that health and wellness has to extend into the workplace, and it's a leader's responsibility to motivate, encourage and enable his or her employees to make healthy choices. 'It all starts with discipline,' Gary said. 'No matter how busy you are, you have to make time. This is too important to your future. Set a goal and start working toward that goal each and every day. It's not easy, but the benefits are tremendous in the long run.'

"I didn't know Gary for long, but it didn't take long to be inspired by his passion for life, his love for his family and the joy and enthusiasm with which he attacked his many projects. I still think of Gary often, and although he's no longer with us, he's still leading by example."

chapter 9

The Power of Relationships

Bill Carteaux, President & CEO, SPI – The Plastics Industry Trade Show Association, was wonderstruck by Gary's ability to pull off the unexpected. In a pinch, Gary could rely on a vast group of friends and acquaintances, ones he treated like family. In return, they always reciprocated.

"I spent the years between 2009 and 2012 out on a limb, with my career at stake, but at least I had good company. Gary Sain was the kind of individual who, when you went into business together, tied his career to yours, and if you were going to go out on a limb, he was going to go with you. To be honest, I haven't known anyone before or since Gary that would be better to have on my side in a situation like the one we were in during those years, as we tried to move a million-plus-square-foot trade show from the city where it was hosted for 39 years to Orlando, Fla., where Gary was head of the tourism board there.

"The name of the trade show was NPE, which originally stood for the National Plastics Exposition, before it was re-branded into NPE: The International Plastics Showcase, and eventually re-re-branded into NPE: The Plastics Show. While at the next show, in 2018, everyone will know NPE as the Plastics Show, in Orlando. Thanks to Gary, our group has always been known simply as 'Plastics.'

"Gary had an affinity for plastics. When NPE first moved to Chicago, way back in 1973, Gary's father was the head of the Chicago Convention & Visitors Bureau. The elder Sain oversaw the transition of NPE into Chicago, and the younger, blessed with tenacity and a unique way of getting things done that's frequently imitated but never replicated, ushered NPE into its new home in Orlando in 2012.

"That this was a family affair from the start was uniquely appropriate, because Gary's brand was such that his business partners, and the people he counted as both friends and colleagues, may as well have been his family. His ability to build relationships throughout his entire career into not just working relationships but real friendships enabled him to draw on those whenever the time arose, as it often did, when he needed to make something impossible possible.

"Gary's brand was one of welcoming tenacity. He was a person who was able to make you feel that you were the most important person in the world to him, but in a way that made it clear that Gary was no pushover. He was as generous of himself as he was savvy in the art of business and marketing. He never failed to deliver something after he'd promised it, and took steps that I still believe, to this day, no one else would've taken to ensure that the plastics industry knew that they were as welcome in Gary's town as they were in their own homes.

"In my role as President & CEO of SPI: The Plastics Industry Trade Association, it's always been part of my job to oversee the production of NPE, with the ongoing support of the NPE Executive Committee. We're an association, and a member-driven one at that, meaning each of our decisions as an organization has to have the approval of the members, as represented by the Executive Committee. And, to put it mildly, throughout the period that Gary and I worked to move NPE from Chicago to Orlando, from the first proposal to the final signature and on to just days before the show opened, the Executive Committee maintained a healthy level of skepticism about the idea. Much of this was justified, and even reasonable, without a doubt, and without the NPE Committee's guidance and involvement, none of these things would've ever come to pass (and I wouldn't ever have gotten to know Gary in the manner I did). Nonetheless, Gary and I knew we were going to be successful, and that was great, but there were a whole host of other people who didn't know that, and some of them were on the NPE Executive Committee.

"Gary's efforts to address the concerns that one NPE Executive Committee member had about Orlando's attractiveness as a business destination offered the purest distillation of his unique brand of customer service, always blended with humor and always carried through to the finish line.

"Gary and I had gotten over almost every hurdle coming down the stretch to move NPE from Chicago to Orlando. We had overcome or addressed every objection, so we thought, but as we were approaching the Fall 2009 SPI Board of Directors meeting where we would eventually make the final decision to move, one Executive Committee member threw out one last Hail Mary concern: 'If we move to Orlando, where am I going to take my customers? Golden Corral?'

"To put this in context, NPE isn't just a chance for plastics companies to network and see the latest technologies in the industry. It's also a chance for companies to spend time with their customers and build their relationships. A lot of times that happens over dinner, and after 39 years in Chicago, many companies knew where their customers liked to go eat, and knew where to take their customers and potential customers depending on the status of the relationship. For them, Orlando was the Wild West. As this particular member suggested, a lot of the board members didn't know enough about Orlando – and its world-class dining options – to make an educated decision about where or how to entertain their customers.

"I shared this with Gary and off he went. Before the board meeting and before the deal to move was officially signed, he flew in to meet this particular board member on his home turf in the Great Lakes region. Gary took him out to dinner and had a conversation with the board member, and then off he went again. This time he arranged a room drop for every SPI board member at our next meeting at the Ritz Carlton in Pentagon City, Va. When they checked in, each of them entered their room to find a box of chocolates, a cordial and their own professionally made menu that, instead of appetizers, salads, entrees and desserts, listed all of Orlando's restaurants and organized them according to things like pricing, which restaurant had the best wine list and other things that a company looking to entertain its customers at NPE might want to know eventually.

"Gary didn't stop with the room drop. He also brought Scott Joseph, Orlando's premier food critic at the time, to the board meeting, along with Orlando's mayor so that they could meet with our board and talk about all the sophisticated and diverse dining options that the city had to offer. After the meeting, during the reception, Gary had even arranged for the governor of Florida at the time to call me personally to talk about all that Orlando had to offer.

"The move to Orlando was finalized at that board meeting, and while I believe that the board members would've agreed to move NPE to Orlando, even if Golden Corral had been the only dining option, they wouldn't have felt as safe and smart and sure of the move as they did because of Gary's ability to bring style and service to everything he did. The board saw firsthand who we were dealing with, and they knew they were in good hands with Gary.

"After the move was finalized, Gary and I were in Orlando one night, along with a group of NPE Executive Committee members, including the one who raised the Golden Corral question in the first place. That day Gary and I assured the board members that this evening we'd be going out to a fancy dinner, a dress-up affair. So, we put on our suits and ties, piled into our limo for the evening and off we went to the restaurant.

"What the group didn't know was that before that night, Gary had reached out to his neighbor and close friend, who happened to own a number of Golden Corral franchises in Orlando. Gary planned a special dinner just for this group of board members and for Mr. 'Where Am I Going to Take My Customers?' in particular. After a short trip, we pulled into a nearby restaurant, bearing a red sign and yellow lettering. It was a Golden Corral, one owned by Gary's neighbor, who greeted us with his wife and daughter before ushering us into a decorated back room and treating us to a marvelous dinner.

"That story epitomizes to me the extent to which Gary would go to drive a point home and to overcome an obstacle, not just because it was overwhelmingly successful, but because it required him to draw on relationships that he had built over the course of his career, and to do it freely and without reservation. He could call on people with ease, because he had dedicated so much to building those relationships that everyone he had worked with – from the owner of Orlando's Golden Corrals to the city government to the airport authority and on down the line – was basically family. When he called on his friends it was less of a business transaction and more of a favor for a beloved family member. Gary had a way of doing that, which enabled him to do things that no one else could, and with an effortlessness that could make you jealous because it made you wonder, 'Why can't all business be like this? Why can't everyone see the value in relationships like Gary can?' His life was a living testament to how much these relationships matter, and tales like the Golden Corral story are the parables leftover to teach us all how to be better business people, and better people.

"What also strikes me about the Golden Corral story and Gary's extra work at the board meeting was that they accomplished more than they initially set out to. The SPI board didn't just come away feeling satisfied with the dining options that Orlando offered potential NPE attendees and their customers. They came away knowing that Gary and his team were the kind of people with whom we could do business. They were the kind of people that kept a sense of humor about things, who lived in the real world and saw every challenge not as an obstacle but as an opportunity, and that kind of thing resonated with the SPI board in a way that I'm not sure much else would have. More than anything, it showed them that, above all, this was fun. Gary and his team were having fun doing all of these heavy lifts to make us feel welcome. They worked hard but enjoyed every minute of it, and it's hard to put into words just how at ease that put the board, and me as well, as the show approached and succeeded mightily.

"As I said, Gary was able to freely call upon the relationships he had built over his career to make what seemed unlikely into something that seemed natural, like it was bound to happen in the first place. One of the reasons why I think we became so close was that our management styles were so similar, which is to say, we both were very collaborative and team-oriented, but very goal-oriented as well. He and I both believed that you build the right relationships, hire the right people, set the expectation and then turn your people loose to let them do it. Gary put his people out front at every turn, bringing them together with my team and letting them do what they needed to do. Part of this is represented in the way that Gary managed the relationship between Visit Orlando (the tourism board led by Gary) and the Orange County Convention Center (OCCC), where NPE was held in 2012 and 2015, and then slated for 2018 and 2021.

"Firstly, I never met an employee at Visit Orlando that didn't love Gary and love his style of management, and I met everyone during those years when we were moving the show. Secondly, it's important for me to note that, in a lot of ways, the OCCC team and the Visit Orlando team all seemed like one team, and that is most certainly not the case in every city. A lot of places can be territorial – some aspects of tourism are covered by the tourism board and others by the convention center – and collaboration seldom occurs except under the most dire of circumstances. In Orlando, under Gary, that was not the case. He knew how vital the OCCC team was to success for the whole city, and so he invested in the relationships necessary to make the two parties work like one well-oiled machine.

"The partnership between Visit Orlando and OCCC was especially seamless, but Gary had built these partnerships all over Orlando in such a way that the entire city seemed as committed to plastics as Gary was.

"Before NPE opened in 2012, a colleague of mine from Italy came up to me at a pre-NPE event and introduced himself to the group I was with and he said, 'It's so cool what you guys did at the airport.' I responded with a blank stare. I was completely unaware that we had done anything with the airport and, more than that, I had no idea what we could have possibly done with the airport that my colleague would be praising. I nodded, pretending to understand, as my colleague explained, 'There was a special line for NPE attendees to get through customs. We didn't have to wait to get through customs if we were here for the show.'

"I played it off like I had known all along, but after the event, I called Gary that night and said, 'Well, you could've at least warned me.'

"Those were the kind of things that Gary did, and was able to do. He rallied the entire community, even the airport authority, to do things that we didn't even request. He brought them on board to support his cause, and that's something that not everyone could do. Even more impressively, it's not something that someone could do and still maintain such positive, beneficial, friendly relationships with the people he needed to help him do it.

"Gary touched so many people in his life, and he was able to bring people together in a way that I've yet to see replicated. I hope that he's remembered for all of his important work, the extent of which I haven't even begun to scratch in this chapter. But I think that if there's one thing he deserves to be remembered for – more than his tenacity, more than the love he bore for his city, more than the way he was able to overcome even the tallest of obstacles in a way that was natural, intelligent, effective and still a ton of fun – it's the fact that Gary was a truly generous individual, mentoring young people coming into his industry and giving back all the knowledge and experience that he had accumulated. His work with the Boys & Girls Clubs, the Rosen school and other venues for mentorship and education is the legacy he's left, in the form of a consummate brand of professionalism that never stresses profit over relationships, yet still manages to be profitable, and that I, personally, strive to replicate every day of my life. In my opinion, a leader is someone who's willing to give everything to the next generation, and even though he's gone too soon, that's what Gary did. People are going to remember him for the contributions he made to the younger generation, and see him reflected in the work they eventually do for the City of Orlando and beyond.

"All of these things, all of these stories and extra steps taken and journeys to that rarely reached realm of above and beyond were aspects of Gary's personal brand: a potent blend of tenacity and commitment to relationships that not only moved one of the country's largest trade shows from its nearly four-decade foothold in Chicago to Orlando, but also changed the lives of hundreds of men and women in the nation's $427 billion plastics industry, including mine. As I said earlier, if there was ever a person to be stuck out on a limb with, I'd want it to be Gary. And his example was one worth striving for, in business and in life. His legacy will be seen in the way that he gave back, and also in the countless lives he touched and in the city he helped lift to a top-tier destination for business travel, in addition to leisure.

"For me, I'll say that I'm a better person for having come into such close contact with Gary and his brand, both as a businessman and just as a man. If you're ever able to summon one-tenth of the energy, care, intelligence, marketing know-how, humility, generosity and just all-around drive that Gary was able to draw upon like Beethoven writing a symphony, give me a call, because I'd like to do business with you, too."

chapter 10

How Do I Want
to Be Remembered?

Joe **Lamond**, President & CEO of the National Association of Music Merchants (NAMM), only knew Gary for a short time. Despite that brevity, Gary left an indelible mark.

  "The fallacy with so many of us is that we think we have forever to complete our life's work, that we'll have time to get it all done. In reality we have today only, and those who truly grasp that concept tend to leave incredible legacies. Gary Sain embraced that concept in his work, in his community and with his family. Some had years of connection and benefited greatly from the interaction. Others, like me, knew him only briefly. But it wasn't the length of time that mattered, it was the impact. The authenticity and clarity of our interactions were remarkably refreshing and made deep impressions. I suspect many others felt the same.

"He left us too soon, and as his family shares the concepts and ideas that Gary lived by, perhaps we will all look at our own lives a little differently and embrace the reality that every moment is an opportunity to make a difference in the world."

From the time Gary and I were married, he always sent quick emails reminding us of our to-do list. Some people might think of that as insulting, but we had so much on our plate, we needed to be reminded. I used to tease him and act as if the Post-it® note that he would leave in the morning got lost. Gary was all about accountability. He was elated once I learned email and texting...now I had no excuse for not following through!

I began to think about all the messages and emails he sent over the years. My kids used to say I had too much in my inbox. Thank goodness I never deleted them because as I went back reading each and every one, things began to become clear. On May 4, 2011, (exactly one year before Gary's death,) he left a profound email. This email might have been a rough draft for an article or interview. In true Gary fashion, he was quick and to the point! This is how it read:

"**Navy family** – uncle as deputy mayor instilled sense of service

Mother – optimism...you can do anything

Father – always tried to meet his expectations

Vanessa and Olivia – their births happiest days of my life

Pam – 30 years of love and partnership

Philosophy – work harder than the next person, be passionate in what you do, give it all you got, never take anything for granted, expect the unexpected

Favorite slogan for kids – choose wisely

What did you give your children? – be versatile, think creatively, never, never have someone tell you you can't achieve, be passionate to those less fortunate, give back to the community and go for your dreams (as long as you have a Plan B)

When I die, how do I want to be remembered? – He gave it his best, he had fun doing it, he used humor as an equalizer, he wanted to win (the right way), he was honest and truthful, he led by example, he loved his family, he made a difference and treated everyone equally

Community service – you have only one life to live. Outside of work and family, give one-third to your favorite charity, one-third to community service and one-third to a service organization. It makes you complete."

As you stop and think about each line in this email, it gives you great insight into who Gary truly was. Who would ever think to do this? These bullet points were key elements through Gary's life. The email did not require a long explanation. It was an outline and short summation of what was important to him. It was a reminder of who he was.

John Morgan, Founder of Morgan & Morgan law firm, looks back at Gary's life balance:

"There are visionaries and vision makers. Some just dream it. Gary Sain did it. Orlando welcomed over 60 million people the last year Gary was among us. That is a staggering number. It is not true that if you build it, they will come. There must be a reason, a message and a hook. Gary gave travelers and visitors around the world the desire to visit Orlando. The competition in the U.S. and the world is intense. Despite the intensity of the competition, Gary found a will and a way to win and, in the process, tourism in Central Florida won.

"At age 61 you are supposed to have a good 20 years left. At least. Or so I hope. But life teaches us there are no sure things and that we never know when our time here will end. Sometimes it comes without warning and it is stunning. Death teaches us what we had and what we will miss and what we will never have again. Things and people we might not think about in-depth until they are gone.

"Gary's death made us think about what we had and what we lost. A family man and a man of the community. A man of ethics and a man of purpose. Life is not all about business, or your family or your community. It is about all three. Gary Sain showed us that every day he got up to greet life. His last steps were taken walking off stage where 900 people had just heard him speak on behalf of all the children who benefit from the Boys & Girls Clubs. Serving his community, promoting his city and making his family proud. Those were his final moments on this earth.

"Great leaders, great husbands and great fathers are impossible to replace, especially to the people who held them so dear. However, their great memories and reputation remain with us always. We will always miss Gary Sain. Yet, we will never forget him. Legends live forever."

We all ponder at some point in our lives how we want to be remembered or what our legacy will be. For some the bar is set very high depending on their goals and vision for the future.

However, ultimately, regardless of what your beliefs are, they usually come down to family, GOD, or spirituality. Some of us are never satisfied. We might continue to keep pushing ourselves to heights we may never have imagined. Our lives never quite turn out as planned. Events and choices we make will continue to change the course we are on and where we will end up. There is always tomorrow. The best thing about a new day is you can always start over.

Family, friends and colleagues view us in a way we would not view ourselves. They see us in a different perspective. We learned this after Gary's passing. It's how we treat others, how we listen, the value of relationships, and the importance of encouragement. These are qualities that you cannot buy. They are deep within us. Some have it and some don't! Your legacy is built on how you approach life, whether it's optimistic or pessimistic.

There is a Native American Proverb that reads: *When you were born, you cried, and the world rejoiced. Live your life in such a way that when you die, the world cries and you rejoice.*

In the Words of Gary's Colleagues and Friends...

"There are a few special times in your professional career when you have the privilege to cross paths with someone who not only influences you; in the case of Gary Sain, someone who became a mentor and friend. Gary had an immediate impact on the Central Florida tourism community when he began his leadership role at Visit Orlando.

"Gary was a leader who didn't let politics, or hidden agendas, get in his way. The way he brought together the tourism community, even competing theme parks and resorts, to truly plow forward as one team was truly remarkable. The Orlando tourism community will be thanking Gary for many years to come. I will be thinking of and thanking Gary as I work every day to live up to his standards."

— **Toni Caracciolo**, Vice President, Marketing & Sales, SeaWorld Parks & Resorts Orlando

---

"Most who knew Gary reflect on his impact on Central Florida in general and Orlando in particular. However, Gary was the type of leader whose influence extends beyond those he directly interacted with. I for one carry his optimistic outlook with me wherever I go. As an international scholar, I was fortunate to have been selected as a two-time Fulbright Scholar (Denmark, 2012 and Austria, 2015), as well as being a visiting scholar in Hong Kong and China.

"After learning of his early passing, I couldn't help but reflect on the stories Gary shared with me and how I'm certain he would have enjoyed knowing his legacy was now being shared in a college classroom halfway around the world through a discussion of social entrepreneurship in the U.S. and abroad. I incorporated Gary's philosophy of listening and mentoring into my Leadership and Strategic Management course section as a way to showcase how positive thinking and innovative leadership can cut across generational as well as cultural barriers. This also aligned perfectly with my responsibility as a U.S. Fulbright Scholar to share the 'American culture and way of thinking' with my hosting universities and communities.

"I realized that Gary Sain had influenced me far more than he could have ever imagined that first day. Here I was, explaining how Gary had taught me that positive thinking wasn't about making you successful, but rather about how positive thinking makes others successful.

> – **Dr. Po-Ju Chen, Ph.D.**, Associate Professor, Fulbright Scholar, Rosen College of Hospitality Management, University of Central Florida

---

"Working my way through college at Georgia State as a front desk clerk at the Omni hotel, I was aware of a new hotel and office complex being built in the suburbs of Atlanta. I wanted desperately to be a part of it, specifically in the sales and marketing area. It would be my first job out of college and I wanted to be a part of the new talk of the town, the Waverly.

"I went on several interviews with clearly not the resume that would fit what they were looking for. I finally made my way to the Director of Marketing, a well-polished, high-energy, fit guy by the name of Gary Sain. He asked some questions about my resume, which I enhanced somewhat, and he seemed to get a chuckle out of it. For example, before being at the front desk at the Omni, I watered plants at the Atlanta Hilton, which was in the engineering department. So I listed myself as a landscape engineer. He said I was creative, and at the end of the interview, I just told him that I really wanted the job, give me a chance and you don't have to pay me much. He called me the next day, gave me that chance, but little did I know the impact that working for Gary would have.

"Immediately, the energy of the hotel and the office took on the personality of Gary's infectious energy and passion. Gary built the brand of the Waverly and the stories that went with it. And that was my first of many lessons I learned: the importance of storytelling, which creates an emotional connection and the 'why' someone should care to be a part of it or engage/purchase it. Today, if I really want to launch a new product, new experience, new employee service initiative, I always try to paint a picture or tell a story to get my point across. And most of the time I am successful as no one was a better storyteller than Gary.

    – **Chuck Bowling**, President & COO,
    Mandalay Bay Resort & Casino

I had the pleasure and honor to get to know Gary personally, as well as through our business ventures. Gary was a legend in this industry, not only in Central Florida but in many other parts of the country. However, I knew Gary in a very different light as our family lived in the same neighborhood. We got to be good personal friends.

"Gary and Pam would constantly open their home to friends and neighbors to celebrate several occasions throughout the year. Gary and I became cycling partners. For quite a few years, we would cycle many, many miles each weekend. We got to know the roads and trails of Central Florida quite well, as well as each other.

"While on our rides, Gary and I had numerous conversations on many subjects, which included business, politics, as well as family. We also spent countless hours talking about our businesses and what factors would make the marketplace successful. It was very intriguing discussing the hospitality industry with Gary, as he was definitely a visionary. This business here in Central Florida grew tremendously due to Gary's ideas, involvement and leadership despite some very challenging economic times. It was through Gary's positive impact that many people succeeded.

"I am personally grateful for the time I got to spend with Gary and am very blessed to have known him. I also am proud to have been able to call Gary Sain a very DEAR friend.
  – **Jim Miller**, retired Vice President, Ecolab, Inc.

One of the things I learned from Gary was to include the next generation of leaders of our industry into the goals of the conference. Because SITE (Society for Incentive Travel Excellence) has the Young Leaders program, I reached out to the chair of the Young Leaders, Cosimo Bruzzese with Briggs in New York. I informed him about my plan to organize a student and Young Leaders conference prior to the SITE conference. We reached out to Abe Pizam, the dean of the Rosen College of Hospitality Management. He agreed soon after our first meeting that he would support this idea and offered us free of charge the meeting space at the college. We had some great speakers at this conference.

"To honor the legacy of Gary as a promoter of our next generation of young leaders, SITE decided to sponsor one student to the Global conference in Orlando, and on June 20, 2012, released this statement:

"'Gary was instrumental in bringing the 2013 Site Global Conference and 40th Anniversary celebration to Orlando. We commit to partnering with the University of Central Florida's Rosen College of Hospitality Management to award one scholarship to the conference in recognition of Gary's leadership and love for the destination and professionals who work there.'"

    – **Joost de Meyer**, CIS, CITE, CMM, ACC,
       Chairman & CEO, First Incentive Travel

"During our Hyatt days when neither of us was traveling, Gary and I commuted to downtown Chicago together. They say if you want to really get to know someone, play golf with them. Try driving into Chicago from 33 miles out every day. He always had a smile, and I don't remember any time when he was 'down.' He was always upbeat. His positive/fun nature, I think, was based on his happiness at home.

"Gary was fastidious about his appearance. Details were important to Gary. He even worked out a plan to prevent wrinkling his tie with his seatbelt during our commute each day. It was a nutty solution, but he had me using the same technique.

"Over time I learned how driven Gary was. During our discussions he would talk about self-improvement, staying in shape (just weeks before he left us, he called and told me he had done 1,200 push-ups that day – his 61st birthday), strengthening his marketing skills and developing other talents. I knew from the beginning that he would never quit working on his leadership and business knowledge until he was a CEO.

"Gary was a natural leader; those on his team and his peers respected him and his ideas. His drive and ambition were very clear. He was on a mission to help his team excel, not simply achieve their goals but to do more. I wouldn't say he was a perfectionist, but he expected people to give their best: Come to work with a great attitude, work hard, create new ideas and when things didn't go as planned, regroup and fix the issues. To my memory, he was not confrontational; he was a coach. On the senior leadership side, he was a great partner. I could count on him giving his frank opinion on all issues facing our team and to help us focus on getting better and making our brand more competitive.

"After Gary left Hyatt, he continued to grow and build his industry network. He was always pushing to find 'better ways,' to help people grow and to help our industry improve and become a bigger influence in America and around the world...and that he did!

> – **Jim Evans**, retired CEO, Best Western International, Jenny Craig International and BRAND USA

Gary Clinton Sain was unlike anyone I have ever met. Gary was the kind of person who would give you a list of 10 things to do and ask you if the first eight were done before leaving the room.

"I came to know Gary when he hired me to be his executive assistant at Visit Orlando. It was a 5-year adventure learning, laughing and growing. Gary had an incredible work ethic and energy, and to work with him required you to have the same. Honestly, his energy was contagious and he was so passionate about his work. He truly loved his job and took the responsibility of marketing Orlando very seriously.

"As much as I cared for him, he was not the easiest person to work with at times, but I enjoyed every moment and I learned a lot.

> – **Marie McLean**, Executive Assistant to the Executive Director, LIFT Orlando

“I knew Gary both professionally and socially. He was the kind of man that you looked up to; the kind of man that everyone wanted to be around. His charitable works, political contributions and civic incentives were just a few of the reasons that kept Gary in the limelight. But what kept Gary in our hearts was his sense of community.

“Every person in Gary's life was important to him, whether it was a family member or an employee he had just met that day. Gary took the time to get to know each and every individual he came in contact with. It was his huge heart that left the biggest impression on us all. He was a man that everyone wanted to know.”

> – **Randy Cook**, Managing Partner,
> Eddie V's Prime Seafood in Orlando

“Gary's idea of writing a book about branding yourself was timely and inspirational to me, especially when I was laid off and became a free bird to provide consulting services to continue doing what I loved to do for so many years – assisting companies to grow their business through international trade and assisting foreign companies to establish and grow their business in the USA.

“Business leaders around the community encouraged me to incorporate my company to start providing consulting services to them.

“While conversing with Gary about my situation during the Air France reception at the Waldorf Astoria Hotel in Orlando, he said: 'Carmenza should be your brand! Your name and personality is the drive for the growth of your company! You love what you do and do it very well, so consider your name or the key letters to create your company.” I came up with 'CZA' for the name of my company. These three letters are always a topic of conversation, which allows me to deliver my elevator speech about what I do. So I think of Gary very often when people ask what CZA means. Thank you, Gary!"

    – Carmenza U. Gonzalez,
      President, CZA, Inc.

"Gary Sain had a profound effect on the Destination Marketing Industry during his tenure as CEO of Visit Orlando. His infectious personality, warm smile, and true concern for people he came in contact with is a rare quality in today's world.

"My story about Gary Sain is a little different from room nights and economic impact within a destination. It has to do with a conversation that we had about extreme heartburn I was experiencing after I ate. This condition had been going on for years. Gary shared with me a story about his father-in-law and the problems that acid reflux can cause. He encouraged me to see a doctor. This conversation took place in July, the year before Gary died.

"After the convention, we went our separate ways and I didn't think much more about it until after Thanksgiving when I decided to schedule a physical at the Mayo Clinic in Jacksonville, Fla. The earliest they could see me was February.

"On New Year's Day, I received a phone call from Gary. He wished me a Happy New Year, and then asked me to report the results from the physical he had advised me to get. After I told him the physical was scheduled for February, Gary laughed and said, 'Good boy ... I'm glad you heeded my advice.' After my physical, the first person I called was Gary to let him know I had not damaged my esophagus with the acid reflux. He was genuinely happy to hear the news.

"Gary's impact on our industry and his love for Orlando will long be remembered. His impact on me, a colleague from Memphis, will never be forgotten."

> **– Kevin Kane**,
> President & CEO, Visit Memphis

"Gary Sain was, without a doubt, the most competitive person I ever met. It didn't matter how substantive – or inconsequential – the challenge or its end achievement might have been. You just knew Gary would HAVE to win. And win at any cost!

"I remember one time we were having lunch or dinner together. I was whining about my lack of discipline when it came to ordering meals and that I had put on quite a few pounds. Gary chimed in that he, too, wanted to lose weight. Now, you have to remember that Gary was ALWAYS in great shape, was a devoted workout guy and, candidly, he never looked like he needed to lose weight. The very next thing out of his mouth was, 'I'll bet you a thousand dollars that I can lose more weight than you.' Taking the bet never crossed my mind because I knew damn well that, if need be, Gary would get himself down to a ghastly 80 pounds for the sake of winning. It wasn't the money; it was the thrill of victory.

"Even though I turned down the bet, Gary knew that he had, de facto, won, and he laughed that cackling laugh of his for at least five minutes. That was just typical Gary behavior."

> **– Jack E. Mannix**, Principal at Mannix & Associates,
> former President & CEO, Ensemble Travel Group

"I had no idea of what an iBRAND was when I met Gary. I soon understood the message: To lead by example, not as a preacher, teacher or world changer. Gary was comfortable in his own skin and wanted you to be in yours.

"I was fortunate to share experiences with him in London, Sao Paulo and many other places that took him out of his comfort zone: cancelled flights, sleeping at airports, lost luggage, no air conditioning, not speaking the language, and the list goes on and on. He was gracious, friendly, and if he was uncomfortable, he sure did not show it. His brand does live on in those places. I miss him every day. iBRAND is a state of mind that everyone should emulate if Gary Sain embraced it."

> – **Jay Santos**, VP of Global Business Development,
> Trend Group of Companies

"Before the 'iBRAND' became a concept, Gary was living the idea of personal branding and all that the concept stood for. He felt and lived out the dictum that 'what you say and what you do should be who and what you are.' You can close your eyes and still see the Gary that became the stuff of hotel stories – enthusiastic, committed to his craft, human in scale, funny, knowledgeable. I was blessed to have him on two of my opening hotel teams, blessed further to have been able to call him and his family my friends."

> – **John LaBruzzo**,
> LaBruzzo Hospitality Advisory Services, LLC

"Most of Gary's calls to me came when he left the Visit Orlando offices to drive home to his girls. The topics ranged from business advice, serving as a sounding board for his ideas, and when he or the organization faced change or a 'crisis.' The calls would last 10 to 30 minutes and were some of the best business strategy conversations.

"One call from Gary came when he was starting at Visit Orlando. He wanted to know did I think it was a good idea for him to buy donuts on Fridays for the staff and deliver them himself. That was absolutely one of the best ideas, simple as it may sound, and fit Gary perfectly. He did something nice for his team; we all like donuts on Fridays, and it forced him to see everyone. How many CEOs say hello to their employees frequently, much less bring donuts?

> – **Bob Wright**, President,
> Vision Marketing & Communications

"I met Gary during a monthly marketing meeting, which I started as the new Director of Sales and Marketing for Hyatt Regency Grand Cypress. Gary was Vice President and the Account Leader for YPB, the agency hired to help us promote the resort. Our objective was to re-establish Hyatt Regency and the Grand Cypress Resort as a world-class resort and the most desirable destination within Orlando for meetings, conventions and leisure guests. Gary and I would start brainstorming and idea dumping on memorable guest experiences and how to promote them. The challenge was to come up with ideas that were unique. Most of the other participants, including myself, would refer to things that we had seen at other properties, which was good but Gary would always say, 'What's unique and different at Grand Cypress? What are we good at and what is available at this resort that isn't available anywhere else?' Gary was a huge champion of branding. It was all about how we as a business and we as people differentiate from others and what we are good at. So as we identified our unique features, amenities and services, it became clear what our objectives should be, and the strategies and tactics we would need to stake our brand claim.

"We went on to launch a couple of really great campaigns, which ultimately led to increased patronage in our restaurants, improved our social banquet F&B (food and beverage) sales and created a much stronger synergy between Hyatt and the Villas of Grand Cypress.

"Through all of this, I learned from Gary how to be more conscious of my own professional and personal brand; that these are really one in the same and the importance of always being true to 'your own brand.'

"I am deeply grateful to have known Gary and spent quality time with him. Through his guidance, I feel I'm a better person, better professional, better leader. I often think about our conversations when I'm confronted with a challenging issue, and the outcome is usually always positive."

　　　– **Bob Dees**, Vice President/Team Director,
　　　ConferenceDirect®

"I first met Gary Sain during a weekend skiing event in Lake Tahoe. He was the new Assistant VP of Sales for Hyatt Hotels. Our wives were also at the event and so we had a brief chance to meet. There was an instant sense of 'ease' when we were together. What was clear to us all was that our values and sense of family were similar.

"At the time that we met, I was the founder and CEO of Conferon, Inc., which was the nation's largest independent meeting planning/consulting firm. Conferon was either rapidly becoming or had become Hyatt's largest purchaser of guest rooms that were associated with meetings. John Leinen was our Hyatt contact during that time period and he received a call from Gary asking for more information about my company and me personally. Gary was interested in growing his and Hyatt's relationship with Conferon and wanted to learn more about our culture and what made us 'tick.'

"John explained to him that our company culture was heavily 'values based' and that the company worked hard to create a sense of family among suppliers, clients and, of course, employees. John also told Gary that I was a passionate Cleveland Indians fan. With that information in hand, he called and invited my family to Chicago for a weekend – with his family!

"Our excited family flew to Chicago, attended a White Sox-Indians game, visited a local theme park with his children and went to his home to have dinner. We never talked business; we only enjoyed our families and learned more about each other.

"That weekend began a long friendship, which was blessed with high levels of trust and a 'more than business' relationship that lasted as long as Gary was alive.

"Gary understood that trust started with sharing similar values and that without trust, real relationships cannot exist. Because we grew to understand one another, we were able to move beyond our business relationship to areas of challenges and shared vision.

– **Bruce Harris**, Executive Director,
    Food2Share, Inc.

Gary Sain Memorial Skybridge

*Naming the bridge that connects my Rosen Plaza
to the Orange County Convention Center after Gary
was a logical tribute to his efforts on behalf of
our convention district community.
Gary really made a difference and his spirit
is alive and well in the Central Florida tourism industry.*

— HARRIS ROSEN,
President & COO,
Rosen Hotels & Resorts

Gary Sain Café

Gary spent countless evenings in the Orange County
Convention Center's Osprey Lounge welcoming guests
or thanking them for their business.
Following Gary's sudden passing it was decided
that we would renovate the lounge and
rename it The Gary Sain Café
as a permanent reminder of his legacy to Orlando
and the Orange County Convention Center.

– KATHIE CANNING,
Executive Director,
Orange County Convention Center

Gary promoting Orlando!

Gathering toys for the Salvation Army Thanksgiving feast.

Gary and Pam

Gary and daughters, Vanessa (left) and Olivia (right)

Gary (right) with his father, Frank Sain (left)

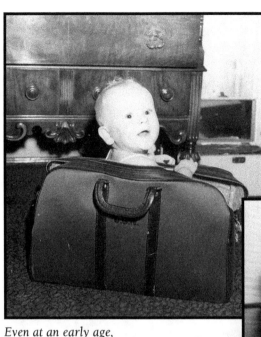

Even at an early age,
travel was in Gary's genes.

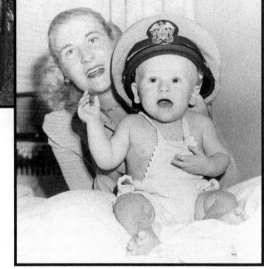

Gary with his mom, Bette

Gary with his mom, Bette, and dad, Frank

Gary as a young boy

*Gary, with mother, Bette,
graduation day from
Davis & Elkins in
West Virginia*

*Pam and Gary,
wedding day,
June 14, 1980*

Olivia and her dad

*Vanessa and her dad
on her wedding day*

If you would like to make a contribution to one of our scholarship funds, please make checks payable to:

UCF Foundation, Inc.

On the memo line, indicate which scholarship:

The Gary C. Sain Memorial Endowed Scholarship or
The Frank C. Sain Memorial Endowed Scholarship

12424 Research Parkway, Suite 250
Orlando, FL 32826